Waterfall Walks and Easy Hikes in the Western Maine Mountains

Doug Dunlap

Chandler Mill Stream Falls

Waterfall Walks and Easy Hikes in the Western Maine Mountains

Doug Dunlap

Down East Books
Camden, Maine

Down East Books

An imprint of The Rowman & Littlefield Publishing Group, Inc.
4501 Forbes Blvd., Ste. 200
Lanham, MD 20706
www.rowman.com

Distributed by NATIONAL BOOK NETWORK

Copyright © 2021 Doug Dunlap

Set in Adobe Minion type by Michael Höhne of Höhne-Werner Design in Wilton, Maine in 2017

British Library Cataloguing in Publication Information available

Library of Congress Cataloging-in-Publication Data available

ISBN 978-1-60893-701-1 (paperback)
ISBN 978-1-60893-702-8 (e-book)

Books in This Series

Day Hiking in the Western Maine Mountains, 2nd Edition
  27 day hikes in the High Peaks and Foothills, ranging from 2.0 to 6.0 miles round-trip, and including level, moderate, and high elevation terrain. *(2015)*

Paddling in the Western Maine Mountains
  22 lake, pond, river, and stream flat water day trips, from short outings of an hour or so, to all day adventures. *(2015)*

Snowshoeing and Cross-Country Skiing in the Western Maine Mountains
  34 forest and lakeside routes, groomed trail systems, mountain ascents— and tips for winter travel on foot. *(2016)*

Waterfall Walks in the Western Maine Mountains
  39 outings—waterfall adventures, foothills and forest hikes, and streamside and lakeside rambles. Most between distances of a half-mile to 2 miles. *(2017)*

Walking Trails in the Foothills of Western Maine
  20 outings—lakeside, riverside, hillside and forest rambles, with waterfalls, mountain views, wildlife watching areas, and choice routes for daily walks. Most distances under 1 mile, many with options to extend. *(2018)*

Table of Contents

Acknowledgements

Michael Höhne and Angela Werner of Höhne-Werner Design bring to their craft a deep love and appreciation for the Western Mountains of Maine. Experts in design, who serve clientele world-wide, they are also avid outdoors people who hike our Maine trails and paddle our waters. I am grateful for the combination they bring of skill and insight. Michael and Angela encouraged me to pursue the writing of a guidebook for visitors to our region of Maine— encouragement that has led to the publication of four books. I thank them heartily and with deep gratitude.

A succession of editors of the *The Franklin Journal*, a county-wide newspaper headquartered in Farmington, have welcomed my column *Foot and Paddle*, which I have had the privilege of writing for nearly 10 years. Some of the entries in this *Waterfalls Walks and Short Hikes...* book have appeared in that column. I thank these editors, who include Mike Petersen, Bobbi Hanstein, Greg Davis, and the current editor, Barry Matulaitis. They have served our Western Maine community with fine vision and a commitment to the outdoor heritage of this magnificent region.

Thank you!

Dedication

My Parents

For those first country walks with my mother, and with my father,

To hilltops, across hayfields, and into the woods,

When I was a boy of 4 or 5 years.

First impressions, long lasting.

Welcome Hikers!

Greetings! I have been hiking the trails of Northern New England for over 40 years. My love of hiking has brought me to the Colorado Plateau and Canyon Lands of the Southwest; to the Alaska Range; to the Appalachians from Georgia to Maine as an Appalachian Trail hiker; to the John Muir Trail in the Sierras of California and the Pacific Crest Trail in Oregon; to Nova Scotia in Canada; and to the Highlands of Scotland. I have led hiking trips as an Outward Bound Instructor, and as a YMCA trip leader. I am a Registered Maine Guide.

For a number of years I have authored a column titled *Foot and Paddle*, for the *Franklin Journal*, a bi-weekly newspaper for Franklin County, Maine. Many of the trail descriptions in this guide first appeared in the *Journal*. As a member of the Sandy River Poets in Franklin County, I put my hiking experiences to poetry.

My family and I are fortunate to live in the foothills of Western Maine, where the nearest forest walk is outside our back door and into the woodlot behind our farm home. From where we have a view in one direction of Mt. Blue, and one of my favorite High Peaks, 4049′ Mt. Abraham (known locally as Mt. Abram, for short), in the other.

Introducing people to the joys of exploring our forests, hills, and high peaks, and of paddling Maine's ponds, lakes, rivers, and streams by kayak and canoe— this is a joy for me. I hope to see you on the trail!

Welcome to some of the most pristine mountain, forest, and lake country to be found anywhere—places of remarkable beauty.

I have personally hiked every trail described in this book—most of them, many times.

--- *Doug Dunlap*

What This Book Contains

Two books in one! (1)A guide to 39 on-foot outings; (2) How to prepare— clothing, gear, food and water, safety planning, weather, hiking with children, hiking with the family dog.

L 39 outings in the foothills of the spectacular Western Mountains of Maine —some of the finest hiking terrain in Eastern North America—in four hiking regions.

L Maine Huts and Trails, Bigelow Preserve, Rangeley Lakes Heritage Trust, Appalachian Trail—these and other trail systems.

L 10 waterfall walks including iconic Smalls Falls, high Angel Falls, Niagara-shaped Grand Falls, popular swimming hole falls at West Mountain Brook and Huston Brook—and a few surprise waters.

L 29 short hikes, most to be hiked in 1–2 hours—some much less—with long views to high peaks, striking streamside or lakeside settings, or the quiet surroundings of the northern forest.

L Hiking tips, clothing and gear lists, safety recommendations, suggestions for hiking with children—and even the family dog.

L Recommended maps and background reading on wildlife, trees, and wildflowers.

L Fresh, detailed account of a walk or hike the author has taken on every trail in the book.

Be Prepared As You Enjoy Your Hike

Even on the short outings described here, and on the relatively moderate terrain associated with most entries in this book, mishaps can occur. A rolled ankle, a tumble followed by a scraped elbow or knee, deep chill from a sudden shower as a weather front moves through—these and other mishaps can happen.

Be prepared to take care of yourself should you have a mishap. Trails are not patrolled. Many hours—even an overnight—may pass before emergency personnel could be notified and arrive to assist. Have the clothing, gear, water, food, and minimum safety preparations to care for an injured person in the field.

See the suggestions in this book for what to wear and what to bring on your outing. Research other sources of your choice for hiking footwear, clothing, gear, food, hydration, trip-planning, and safety information. Complete a first aid course. Take a course in outdoor skills.

New to outdoor life? Consider a guided hike at first, led by a Registered Maine Guide.

The descriptions herein are good faith accounts of the author's personal experience. Experiences of others will vary. Entries in this book include outings at commercially-owned or operated areas, state parks and public lands, not-for-profit organizations, and on private property—each of which has its own policies and procedures for trail access, maintenance, and oversight. The possibility exists of the closing of a trail, and changes to—among other things—approach roads, trail locations, the nature of a route or trail, services and amenities, and fee structures.

Always inform a responsible person in writing of your hiking plans, and when you expect to return.

Happy Trails!

Why This Book?

Welcome to this book of waterfall walks and short hikes! Or, more accurately, to this *land apart* of waterfalls and short hikes! The Western Mountains of Maine offer some of North America's most pristine and approachable forest and mountain terrain.

For all those who welcome a short outing—a short time apart—this book is for you! What is it that you seek? A waterfall plunging into a broad pool or tumbling through a rock chute; or a pine and fir encircled forest glen, a streamside rock, or lakeside beach; or a rock perch open to a panorama of Maine's High Peaks—any of this on not too far a hike?

Perhaps you seek a refreshing walk to start or to end the day. Maybe you wish to begin a hiking habit, for yourself, or with others. Short outings are a good way to start.

Whatever beckons you to a short walk—welcome!

Short?

Of the 10 waterfalls described, 8 involve walks of 2.0 miles or less round-trip. The 29 short hikes are of similar length. All but one are 2.0 miles or less, and the one—along the east shore of Flagstaff Lake to Flagstaff Hut, is over fairly even ground.

At a pace of 2 miles per hour, most hikes may be completed in one hour or less. If your pace is slower—or faster—plan accordingly. Of course, there is no rush, and most hikers will want to plunk themselves down in an inviting spot to watch, listen—or do nothing!

To help you to select your hikes, I list the elevation gain for every outing; and I provide a first-person account of a recent hike I have taken on each trail. Remember—I have hiked every one of these trails, and more than once!

Looking for a Longer Hike?

For those who seek longer hikes, see my companion book *Day Hiking in the Western Mountains of Maine, Second edition* (2015). The 27 hikes in that Day Hiking book include approaches to all four Maine Huts and Trails Huts in operation at this writing; the 4000' peaks of Saddleback, Saddleback Horn, Sugarloaf, North and South Crocker, and West Peak and Avery Peak in the Bigelow Range.

At a bit lower elevation are other peaks on the Bigelow Range—North and South Horn, Cranberry Peak, and Little Bigelow. More hikes: north-lying Snow Mountain; west-lying West Kennebago and Low Aziscohos; Bald Mountain in Oquossoc; and the Weld area peaks in the Tumbledown Range and Mt. Blue. The popular Appalachian Trail route to Piazza Rock is in this collection. Other trails include the new north-south Fly Rod Crosby Trail on the south slope of the Saddleback Range.

To minimize duplication, while being thorough and faithful to the theme of the book in your hands, I include three outings from the *Day Hiking* book in this *Waterfalls Walks and Short Hikes* book: *South Poplar Stream Falls*, as it is a waterfall of remarkable beauty; *Rock Pond Trail*, because it is a short, water-accessing trail on the north slope of the Saddleback Range; and *Flagstaff Lake East Shore to Flagstaff Hut*, as it is a short, level route, consistent with the terrain and distance contained in the *Waterfall Walks and Short Hikes* volume.

Readers who have both books will notice that I have prepared distinctive descriptions for these hikes with the particular audience for each book in mind. Further, I re-hiked the above trails in preparation for this new book in order to bring fresh observations for those out for a short walk or hike.

Enjoy your hike! Start a family hiking tradition! Introduce a friend to walking in the forest and foothills, and by our lakes and streams. Welcome to the Western Mountains of Maine!

--- *Doug Dunlap*

You are in Hiking Country!

Franklin County, Maine, and adjacent regions, are home to 10 of Maine's 14 peaks that surpass 4000' in elevation—we call our backyard *Western Maine's High Peaks Region.* Here find major trail systems such as the Appalachian Trail, Maine Huts and Trails System, Bigelow Preserve Trails, Northern Forest Canoe Trail, Arnold Trail, Fly Rod Crosby Trail, and dozens of local trails. Expansive lakes, wild rivers, countless backcountry streams and ponds—all here!

Outings in this book are readily reached from High Peaks towns such as Rangeley, Stratton, Kingfield, Phillips, and Weld. Lodging, campsites, restaurants, outfitters are here to serve you. Gateway communities of Farmington and Wilton offer further options as a base of operations.

Plan your stay by contacting:

🥾 Franklin County Chamber of Commerce
www.franklincountymaine.org/
🥾 Maine High Peaks
info@maineshighpeaks.com
🥾 Maine Huts and Trails
www.mainehuts.org
🥾 Rangeley Lakes Chamber of Commerce
www.rangeleymaine.com

If you enjoy hiking, this is the place to be! If you are new to hiking, your "trail" to the fine outdoor sport of hiking starts here—in the Western Mountains of Maine!

Abbreviations

You may encounter these in the book, or in the field.

BPL: Bureau of Public Lands (Maine)
MATC: Maine Appalachian Trail Club
MHT: Maine Huts and Trails
RLHT: Rangeley Lakes Heritage Trust
RLTC: Rangeley Lakes Trails Center
SOC: Sugarloaf Outdoor Center
USGS: United States Geological Survey (Maps)

Words to the Wise

L *Trail Conditions and Walking Pace:* Expect everything from level, leaf-littered trails, to rocks, roots, and occasional mud (enhanced by animal tracks!). The glaciers had a lot to do with it! Those masses of ice retreated 11,000 years ago, shaping the landscape. Streams and rivers carved ways down the mountain's sides. Results? The remarkable sculpted terrain of Western Maine.
Expect to take a bit more time when hiking this terrain, as compared with more level ground.

L *Mountains make their own weather:* Have clothing and gear suitable for sudden weather changes—such as fast moving electrical storms in summer, or a cold front that causes the temperature to drop precipitously in minutes. I carry a waterproof jacket, doubling as wind breaker on most hikes, and often another warm layer. Be alert to weather forecasts. Particularly on longer hikes, carry additional layers for warmth and for wind and rain protection. See more suggestions for clothing and gear later in the book!

L *Water:* Carry drinking water—enough for both the hike in and the return hike. Treat all water in the back country (streams, ponds, springs) by filtering, use of chemical purifiers, or other effective means. Clarity of water and distance from roads and dwellings is no guarantee of water purity.

L *Trail maintenance:* Much trail clearing and upkeep is the work of volunteers. Spring particularly is a busy time for trail work, as winter storms and spring run-off may cause damage to a trail. If you encounter a need for maintenance such as a footbridge washed away, or a fallen tree blocking the trail, make an effort to report the situation—contact the trail maintaining organization or property overseer mentioned in this book.

L *Inform others of your plan:* Always let someone know where you are going and what time you expect to return.

Trail Distances

Trail distances described in this guide are usually those provided by the organization that maintains the particular trail. Trail signs, maps, and published guides are among the sources.

Is the distance on a sign different from that on a map?

Different organizations use different methods for measuring trails, such as measuring wheels, GPS, map measurement, and walking pace. Expect variation between what is listed in this book, or other books, maps, and signs.

When variation does occur, it likely will be minimal, particularly for the short outings in this book.

When no mileage information is available from an organization, I provide an estimated length.

What Are You Wearing? — What Is in Your Daypack?

For short outings a few simple essential items may suffice. Fine tune the list to fit the outing. What you carry on a waterfall walk may differ from what you bring on a forest walk. Be alert to factors that would require certain items, and specialized items—changing weather, time before darkness, remoteness of trail.

What to Wear

____ Hiking shoes. What is on your feet should provide good grip, and stability. For short hikes athletic shoes may be fine. But be aware that Maine trails can be muddy, even on dry days in summer, and choose footwear accordingly. Blisters occur when footwear and feet are new to one another! Break-in new shoes for at least one week before trail-hiking.

____ Socks: wool or wicking synthetic material.

____ Shorts or hiking pants, quick-drying.

____ Shirts: Short and long sleeve, depending upon weather; quick-drying.

____ Warm layer for high ground or by a lakeshore, where winds may create cold conditions on a mid-summer day. Fleece or long-sleeve t-shirt of wool or poly-material.

____ Light-weight rain jacket which may double as a wind-breaker.

____ Sun hat

____ In cool weather, stocking cap and gloves or mittens; balaclava or neck gaiter for cold weather. These can be handy on high ground and by lakeshores even in summer.

What to Carry in Your Day Pack

___ Map: See entries for suggested maps. Be certain that you can locate yourself on the map—i.e. that you know where you are.

___ Water—sufficient for the hike up or out, *and the return.* A one liter container will usually suffice. For unusually hot or humid days, pack additional water. (Also leave water in your vehicle for all members of the hiking party at the end of the hike.) Carry a water purification means (filter, or chemical treatment, for example) if your hike will be an extended one, and if you will be near water, and one liter may not be enough.

___ Sustaining lunch/ snack foods.

___ Small trash bag. Leave no trace, no wrappers, no orange peels—nothing, please.

___ Sun protection: Sun screen, lip balm, bandanna, sun glasses.

___ Insect repellent. Covering with clothing is advised. If you use repellent, keep away from nylon and plastics, and apply with back of hand to avoid eye contact. Lotion is more efficient than spray—and keeps you and your companions from breathing spray.

___ Biodegradable toilet paper and hand sanitizer.

___ Notebook, sketchpad

___ Guides to wildflowers, birds, trees, mammals

___ Trekking poles or hiking staff: Good for balance and saving wear/tear on lower body; especially useful for stream crossings, and for occasional steep step-downs.

___ Water shoes or sandals to change into for wading in a stream pool or lake, where the bottom may be rock or mud.

___ Towel (small pack towel, or an extra bandana or two, may be all that is needed).

A Pack Within the Pack — My *Ready Bag*

I carry a small waterproof bag inside my day pack—my *ready bag*. It contains items that I may not need on most hikes, but when I need them—I really need them! These take up little room, and do not weigh much.

At some point in my hiking career, I *have* needed each item on the list!

___ Headlamp with fresh batteries *and* spare batteries—*even if no expectation to be out after dark.*

___ "Space blanket": Reflective, heat-retaining blanket. These fold to the size of a wallet.

___ Compass (If contained within a battery-powered device, such as a phone or GPS unit, carry a separate compass in event of battery drain.)

___ Fires starter: waterproof matches, lighter, or both.

___ First aid supplies: Think rolled ankle, scraped knee, elbow, or hand; blisters: Band-aids, antiseptic, blister treatment, tape to wrap a rolled ankle.

___ Small knife

___ Whistle: a default communication device if someone gets separated from the party, or has a mishap.

___ Spare warm socks: I have used these as mittens in suddenly cold weather; and as water shoes to take a dip in a rocky stream; or as spare socks!

___ 1-2 bandanas: many uses.

___ Water purification tablets

___ Notebook/pencil

On the Day of Your Hike

Start with ample time to return before dark: Early starts provide opportunity to see wildlife, to spend extra time if you wish, and to have ample time before dark if someone in the group is moving slowly.

Leave a written note with a responsible person. Describe where you are going and when you plan to return.

The right gear: Confirm that each person has the necessary gear, food, water, clothing, and footwear.

Food and water for afterwards: Set aside water and food to be left in the vehicle for the return at the end of the hike.

Tell each person in your hiking party:
- Where the hike leads
- Length of trail
- Estimated time for the hike out and back.

On the Trail

For groups, even on a short hike, have *a lead hiker* and *a sweeper hiker* (at the end of the group). All other hikers walk between these two. No one runs on ahead. No one is left behind.

Never split the party. In the event of an injury or illness there may be no way to communicate to others if the group has divided. *Never leave someone behind who is to catch up later.*

A hiker who is moving slowly will travel more quickly in the supportive conversational company of others.

A slow steady pace, even if it is quite slow, is much less tiring than frequent starts and stops.

Turn Around Time

In every hiking season some hikers get caught out after dark, unexpectedly. Setting a *Turn Around Time* reduces the chance that darkness will fall before a party returns.
- Count the number of hours from the start time to sunset.
- Divide that number in half.
- Add this half to the start time.
- This is your turn-around time—the time to turn back, regardless of whether you have reached your goal for the hike.

Example: You start a hike to a waterfall at 6:00 p.m. on a July evening. Sunset is 8:12. Amount of time to sunset is 2 hours, 12 minutes. Half of that is 1 hour 6 minutes. Add that to 6 p.m. to get 7:06. The "Turn Around Time" for your hike is 7:06 p.m.

Lost?

Becoming lost on the short trails described in this book would be quite rare. However, it is a good idea for those who hike to have an understanding of what to do when lost.

- If you are lost: *Stop walking. Sit down.*
- Look in the direction from where you have come for a trail marker or blaze.
- Attempt to contact your party by cell phone. Text may work where voice does not.
  If time passes, attempt to contact 911, giving location as best you can, noting landmarks you can see, or recently passed. Locate yourself on your map.
- Each person in the Maine woods should carry a whistle.
  Whistles may be heard at a far greater distance than the human voice.
- Signal with the whistle as follows:
  One blast = "Here I am." (usually this is the only signal necessary)
  Two blasts = "You walk to me."
  Three blasts = "Emergency! Get here by the quickest means!"
- *Help yourself to be found.* Signal with the whistle. *Make yourself visible*—get into an open area. Build a safe fire. Maintain it as a signal, night and day.
- Keep warm and dry using the extra layers you have packed, and the "space blanket".
- Eat from your spare food. Keep hydrated. Gather dry firewood to maintain your fire, and for exercise and morale.
- Most lost persons are found within 48 hours, especially if they have left a written note of their plans with a responsible person and that person contacts authorities.

Dogs

I enjoy bringing our Labrador Retriever—leashed—on many hikes, but not all. Dogs, like people, do best when they gain some conditioning, and some experience with the sights and sounds—and smells—of the mountains. Introduce your dog to hiking, to other hikers, and to other dogs on trail, by practicing near home before taking a mountain hike.

- Some terrain—mud, rock—will be difficult on your dog's feet. I have seen dogs just quit, lie down, and refuse to move on. Can you carry your dog down a mountain?
- With a dog in the woods, there is little chance that you will see wildlife. Ground-nesting birds such as ruffed grouse will be in extreme danger. Mammals, from squirrels to white-tailed deer, will head for seclusion.

- Territoriality: You know about this from walks in your home neighborhood. On trail, whose territory is it when two (or more) dogs meet? Or the dog encounters children and adults new to the dog? Avoid putting your dog under territorial stress.
- Leashing: Admittedly, leashing can be a sensitive subject for dog owners, who consider their pet to be under voice control. Consider that a forest environment has many distractions (usually new scents) for a dog, and that dog behavior in the Maine woods may become very different from that at home or in other familiar environments. I have encountered dogs that ran from their owners, chasing deer, and traveled many miles from where their owners last saw them. At least twice in my experience the disappearance occurred on a Sunday afternoon hike, the dog could not be located by nightfall, and adults in the family had to report for work out-of-state the next day. What a quandary!
- Above tree line dogs are to be leashed. At high elevations birds and small mammals have their homes near ground level, and have no protection for themselves and their young against a curious dog.
- Clean up after your pet near water. Please.

Children

Children love to hike!

Suggestions:

- Build success into the hikes—particularly the first few. Keep it short and simple, and memorable. Walk to a spot with a distinguishing feature—a long view, a lakeside spot, or a waterfall.
- Better to have a child say "I want to go on a longer hike next time," than to say "That hike was too long. I don't want to go hiking again."
- Give the child the opportunity to carry a pack, even if very light and containing something as simple as a jacket or snack. This is not a deal-breaker, but they may enjoy carrying something. The best packs have a waist belt and do not flop around and become unwieldy. If buying a new pack seems costly, check local thrift shops. (I have bought brand-name children's packs for a dollar!)
- Sketch-pads and journals work well with kids. Give them a chance to sit in the woods or at a viewpoint, and record what they see and hear. You may be amazed!
- Wildlife, trees, and flowers. Look at pictures before the hike.

- Music: Leave recorded music at home. For many families this is a hiking rule. Children will get used to it! Invite them to listen to the sounds of the forest.
- New to hiking? Prepare for your upcoming hike by walking the same distance as the trail on level ground—such as on a back road near home, or in a park—before hiking that same distance up a mountain and back.
- Tell children how far you are going and how long it is expected to take. This can limit the "Are we there yet?" question.
- Maintain photo albums of your hikes, and display your child's sketches, perhaps a quote from a journal. Celebrate that time in the outdoors!

Water

- All back country water should be treated before drinking.
- Water that looks clear is not necessarily safe to drink.
- Treatments include: water filter, water purification tablets, or boiling.

Sanitation

Toileting:
- Please step *well off* the trail.
- Dig a hole in the ground with your boot.
- Deposit biodegradable toilet paper in the hole.
- Cover.

Please, please, do not litter the forest with toilet paper.

Cell Phones

Kindly understand that many hikers seek out the forests, mountain tops, and wild waters in order to enjoy the sounds of the wind, and the birds—and even the sound of silence. Think concert hall or house of worship.

As a courtesy to other hikers, kindly keep your phone turned off, or place on Airplane or Reduced Battery Load modes. This is also a good move to conserve battery power for a true emergency.

If you must make a call, please move to an area well beyond earshot of other hikers.

In many of the remote areas in this book, there may be no reliable cell phone service. Using Airplane or Reduced Battery Load modes will prevent the phone from using up battery life searching for a signal.

Care for the phone as an emergency device.

GPS

While GPS devices have become common among hikers, outdoors-people have traveled quite well for centuries (millennia) without them. I have them, but always carry a paper map on my hikes. Why so? It is a good practice to see features of the terrain around me, and to anticipate the terrain to come. Maps help me to do that. I can look out from a viewpoint, see a ridge, or a stream valley, and place myself on the map. At any given point on a hike, I seek to be able to pull out my map and say "There—we are right about there."

If you have a GPS unit, use it to learn to read the landscape. In that way, if the GPS should run out of battery life, you—armed with that paper map and your ability to read the landscape—will know where you are.

Trails in Winter

Some of the trails in this collection are readily accessed in winter—but others are not because of remoteness, unplowed roads and parking areas, sections prone to icing, and complex water crossings.

Winter travel by foot requires particular types of trip preparation, safety and self-rescue considerations, clothing, gear, food, and arrangements for drinking water. Hike with a person experienced in winter travel.

When considering winter use of a hiking trail, consult with a knowledgeable source about the nature of the trail in winter, and current conditions.

I have published *Snowshoe and Cross-Country Ski Outings in the Western Mountains,* Foot and Paddle Publications, 2016 for those who seek the serenity and wild beauty of the Maine mountains in winter. The book provides detailed descriptions of winter hikes—and a guide to winter hike preparation.

Trail Organizations Mentioned in this Guide

Maine Appalachian Trail Club (MATC). www.matc.org. P.O. Box 283 Augusta, ME 04332. Maintains the Appalachian Trail in Maine from Grafton Notch northeast of Bethel, to Mt. Katahdin. The MATC is not a hiking club—although its members surely love to hike—but rather a group of volunteers who maintain the Trail such as by cutting fallen trees and encroaching brush, marking the way, and maintaining shelters along the route.

Maine Bureau of Parks and Lands. www.maine.gov/doc/parks/ Oversees Maine Public Lands and Maine State Parks, including Bigelow Preserve, Mt. Blue State Park, and land in vicinity of Smalls Falls.

Maine Huts and Trails. www.mainehuts.org; 207-265-2400. Year-round trails, groomed for cross-country skiing in winter, and maintained for three-season hiking, connecting back country lodges offering meals and overnight accommodations. Reservations required for overnight stays.

Rangeley Lakes Heritage Trust: www.rlht.org; 207-864-7311. The Trust maintains a number of trails in the Rangeley Region, and manages the Cupsuptic Campground west of Rangeley on Cupsuptic Lake.

Guide to Entries

Overview: Distance, terrain, highlights such as views, streams and waterfalls, lakeshore; nature of the forest growth.

Trailhead: Point where the trail begins; and driving directions.

Nearest town: Closest town(s) that offer food and gasoline.

Maps: *Maine Atlas* Map #: Refers to the *Maine Atlas and Gazetteer* published by Delorme, Inc. of Freeport, Maine. This is a widely used resource in Maine.

Trail Maps: Local or regional maps such as those of Maine Huts and Trails, Rangeley Lakes Heritage Trust, or the trail centers at Rangeley Lakes Trails Center or Sugarloaf Outdoor Center.

USGS: United States Geological Survey Maps. These are available in local sporting goods stores, major outdoor retailers, www.usgs.gov and various software programs.

Elevation Gain: One indicator of trail difficulty.

On Trail: Account of one or more hikes the author has taken on this trail.

Locator Map: Indicator for driving access, trailhead location, and general trail route. The scale is such that these are not intended for navigation. Rather, they provide a visual overview of trail location.

Locator Map Legend

This is the legend for the maps in this book:

━━━━ Paved Road	- - - - - Unpaved Road	
──── Main Trail	- - - - - - Alternate Trail	
P Parking Area	Waterfall	

Rangeley-Saddleback Region

Famous for the high, glacier-scoured Saddleback Range and for the expansive Rangeley Lakes Chain; the Rangeley Region also offers many a short foothills hike at low elevations—some near the shores of Rangeley Lake, and others in the foothills north and south of the Saddleback Range.

Three of Western Maine's most popular waterfalls are here—Angel Falls, Cascade Gorge, and Smalls Falls—and the not-so-well-known Chandler Mill Stream Falls, a striking gorge only a few steps from Smalls Falls. The Rangeley Lakes Heritage Trust maintains a series of short hiking paths along the north shore of Rangeley Lake, and by the Rangeley River—each with a different set of views. The Organon Trails—and the Tim Baker Nature Trail (great for kids or the young at heart of any age), add to the opportunities.

Two of Western Maine's birding trails—Mingo Springs and Perham Stream— and the popular Daggett's Rock walk and the Orbeton Stream Conservation Area in the foothills south of Saddleback, round out the list of beckoning trails!

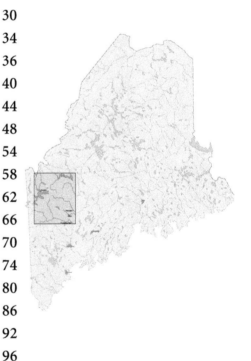

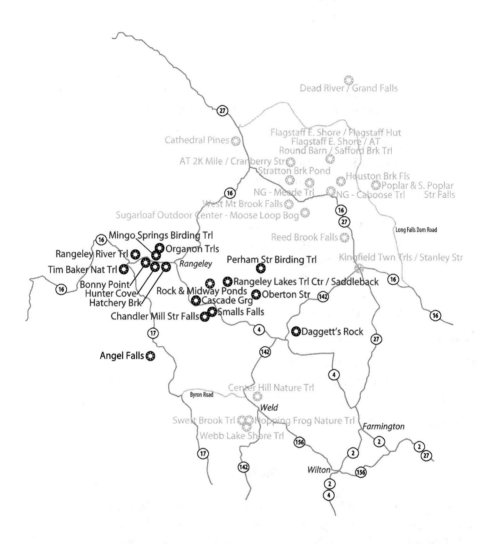

Dead River / Grand Falls

27

Flagstaff E. Shore / Flagstaff Hut
Cathedral Pines
Flagstaff E. Shore / AT
Round Barn / Safford Brk Trl
AT 2K Mile / Cranberry Str
Stratton Brk Pond
Houston Brk Fls
NG - Meade Trl
NG - Caboose Trl
Poplar & S. Poplar
Str Falls
16
West Mt Brook Falls
Sugarloaf Outdoor Center - Moose Loop Bog
16
27

Long Falls Dam Road

Reed Brook Falls

Mingo Springs Birding Trl
16
Organon Trls
Rangeley River Trl
Perham Str Birding Trl
Kingfield Twn Trls / Stanley Str
Tim Baker Nat Trl
Rangeley
16
Bonny Point
Rangeley Lakes Trl Ctr / Saddleback
16
Hunter Cove
Rock & Midway Ponds
Oberton Str
142
Hatchery Brk
Cascade Grg
Chandler Mill Str Falls
Smalls Falls
16

17
4
Daggett's Rock
27

Angel Falls
142

4

Center Hill Nature Trl

Byron Road
Weld

Sweet Brook Trl
Hopping Frog Nature Trl
Farmington
Webb Lake Shore Trl
2
2
17
156
27
142
2
Wilton
156
2
4

Cascade Gorge

Rangeley Lakes Heritage Trust
Sandy River Plantation

Overview: Rangeley Lakes Heritage Trust. 0.5 mile (1.0 mile round-trip) trail over rising, occasionally rocky, terrain to the gorge of Cascade Stream, tumbling down the west slope of the Saddleback Range. Swift-running waters race over short, impressive drops, to set up a continuous roar. Elevation gain: 300' to top of the gorge. Good spot for lunch—or to linger for a few hours to watch the waters roil, and listen to the tumble, rush and roar through the gorge.

Trailhead: Cascade Gorge Road, 0.1 mile off Maine Highway 4, opposite the junction for the South Shore Road (Road to Rangeley State Park) 3 miles south of downtown Rangeley. Another entrance is 0.1 miles north of this junction, on Route 4. These short roads do not appear on the Delorme *Maine Atlas* map, but are marked with road signs. Parking is up a short, steep driveway (Rangeley Lakes Heritage Trust sign).

Nearest Town: Rangeley

Maps: Delorme *Maine Atlas* Map #28, 5-E (lower edge); (Cascade Gorge Road and Trail not on map, but Cascade Stream is shown.); Rangeley Lakes Heritage Trust Map: www.rlht.org. USGS: Rangeley

Elevation Gain: 300' maximum to head of gorge

On Trail:

Looking for a short hike? A hike to start the day, provide a lunch spot, offer an evening outdoor opportunity, or to introduce children to hiking? Cascade Gorge in Sandy River Plantation, south of Rangeley, is a good choice. A half mile of hiking provides outstanding views of a series of waterfalls and chutes on Cascade Stream, and travel through a fine mixed growth forest. On a sunny day you might want to take a dip in the stream!

At midday my hiking companions and I enjoy lunch next to a thundering waterfall on Cascade Stream as a ruby-throated hummingbird hovers over rolling water 10 feet away. Was it attracted by the glint of the sun on the splash off

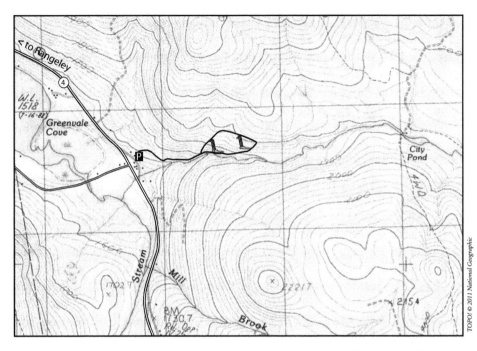

the falls? Dampened rock moss glistens on stream-side boulders. Bunchberries are everywhere—in their bright red, full-fruited stage. In the shade a red mushroom stands bright as a flower. An old apple tree, perhaps the product of browsing deer, has tumbled green apples from a small meadow toward the stream. Barely ten minutes of hiking brings me to this idyllic spot.

Cascade Stream flows out of Eddy Pond on the western slope of Saddleback Mountain, one of Maine's great high peaks, at 4116' elevation. This wild mountain stream twists, plunges, rolls, thunders, rattles through a winding, rocky gorge near the base of the mountain before flowing quietly under Maine Highway 4 to be joined by Long Pond Stream and flow into Rangeley Lake at its southeast cove. Most people drive by without knowing that this gem of a hike is just off the highway. I know that was the case for me until I learned about the trail from folks at the Rangeley Lakes Heritage Trust which owns the land and maintains the trail. Cascade Gorge is on the Maine Registry of Critical Areas, which means that it has precious and unique wild features—all the more reason to take the hike!

To reach Cascade Gorge from the south, follow Highway 4 towards Rangeley into Sandy River Plantation. Pass Beaver Mountain Pond on the left, and look for the South Shore Road, also on your left—indicated by a sign for Rangeley Lake State Park. Immediately across from the South Shore Road, on the right, is the Cascade Road. Turn right, go 100 feet; turn left onto the Town Hall Road, so named because the town office for Sandy River Plantation is on this road, not far from the trail itself. A Rangeley Lakes Heritage Trust sign points the way to a steep gravel drive that leads to a small parking lot. If coming from Rangeley, after crossing the town line from Dallas Plantation to Sandy River Plantation, watch for the South Shore Road on your right. Take a left onto Cascade Road. If you refer to the Delorme *Maine Atlas*, Map 28, the South Shore Road is clearly indicated, but the Cascade Road does not appear on the map.

The trail, marked by both red metal disks and arrows, and white paint blazes, begins at the south side of the parking area. Our hiking party steps into the woods, which here are thick with young fir, and we are on our way. After a short ascent, we scramble over a rough ledge outcrop, watch our footing, and emerge from the woods to flat ledge rimmed by reindeer lichen. Beyond that lies a meadow under a power line. A side trail leads west (right) to a set of falls. The stream may also be reached by turning right to walk on the power line to descend to the stream below. Either of these routes may be difficult, depending upon the water level. We choose to continue on the main trail.

Heading southward, crossing under the power line, we follow the main trail as it parallels the stream, and ascend the slope on the east side of the gorge. We are within 50' of the stream. The cool air fills with the thunder of the cascades. We see frothing, roiling white water through gaps in the trees, and follow a short side trail to the stream bank for a close look. The falls tumble into a pool, where the water looks strangely still—then empties out of the bottom edge of the pool to drop, rumble, and once again, fall out of sight. Shall we stop here? The waters roar above this point. There is more to these falls upstream! Off we go.

At one point a set of rock steps, constructed by the Maine Conservation Corps in 2003, helps us negotiate a short pitch. A wood railing has been added in the years since. In the dappled light under high hemlock and fir that border the trail, the pathway has a cathedral-like feel. We find many a viewpoint along the way—some to overlooks of more cascades; some leading to the edge of pools that under the right conditions might offer a dip.

We use care when we approach the edge of the gorge at any point along the trail. The cascading water throws spray up and onto the surrounding rock, rendering them quite slippery. *A fall here could result in serious injury. Use care.*

Near the upper end of the falls a trail intersection offers a choice. To the right a trail continues along the gorge to a set of steps and a plank fence overlooking the uppermost falls. This section of trail is rough, and crosses a muddy seep. Just beyond the fence the trail ends at a perch above this last of falls.

The trail to the left ascends steeply, climbing a bluff above the stream, which is no longer in view—but still quite loud. In 100 feet a blue-blazed boundary line intersects the trail. Although a worn path continues upstream in the undergrowth, there are many fallen trees blocking the path, and some new growth makes the way obscure. We have reached the top of the gorge—better to turn around at this point!

We spend one hour on our round trip Cascade Gorge Trail hike. The trail could be covered in half that time, but why rush? I lost count of the number of falls, and of the number of pools, too! This is a good trail for lingering!

On my hike we meet visitors from North Carolina, Tennessee, and New York—and a local family who have come to spend most of the day. Franklin County's trails are a major attraction for visitors, and in the back yard for locals! The next time you are driving to or from Rangeley, stop by Cascade Gorge!

Smalls Falls

Maine Public Reserved Land
Letter E Plantation

Overview: Short, 0.1 mile walk to lowest of four pools at foot of five-story gorge in the Sandy River. Upper pools reached by crossing a footbridge to ascend a 0.1 mile trail along the west bank of the gorge, where a fence lines the edge of the gorge. (Round-trip 0.4 miles). Picnic area, outdoor grills, toilet. Maine Department of Transportation Rest Area.

Trailhead: West side Maine Highway 4 in Letter E Plantation, north of Madrid; south of Rangeley. Prominently signed. Drive in 0.1 mile on signed driveway to parking and picnic area. Trail starts at north end of parking area where a footbridge crosses the Sandy River. First, lower, pool is immediately upstream from bridge. Trail to upper falls continues at west end of bridge, turning right (upstream) to parallel the river. Lunch, swim or dip or wade at the lower pool; explore upstream pools, choosing the extent of outing that fits your interest.

Nearest Towns: Rangeley (north); Phillips (south).

Maps: Delorme *Maine Atlas* Map #19, 1-A. The Smalls Falls Rest Area appears on many state highway maps. USGS: Jackson Mountain

Elevation Gain: *Descend* 20' to lower pool; Ascent: 200' gain to upper falls.

On Trail:

Spring—the time of year when the rivers run high with melt from the winter snow pack! Time to head for Smalls Falls—although, truly, I do come to the falls year-round, including winter. Shady coolness and refreshing waters in summer, foliage-lined banks in fall, natural ice-sculptures in winter, rushing runoff in spring—there is a continually compelling spot! I choose a midweek afternoon for a walk to the falls.

Only one other vehicle is in the parking area. At high summer, this is a popular spot—for picnickers, photographers, artists with canvas and oils or watercolors, and many a family here for a dip in one of the many pools.

The trail is well-marked, leaving from the north end of the parking area to cross a 30' bridge over the Sandy River. The lower falls stand in full view from

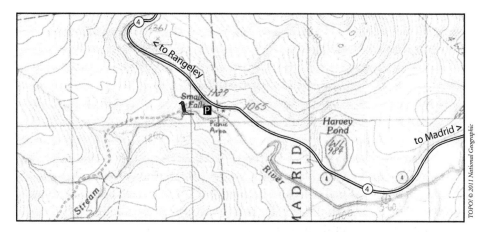

the bridge, angling in from the right, dropping left, tumbling into the great pool immediately upstream from the bridge. This lowest pool may reached from the side of the bridge near the parking area.

Once across the bridge I turn right, to follow the well-worn path up the west bank of the river. A fence stands between the steep and slippery west bank, and the path—do stay behind the fence! Some portion of the long continuous set of falls is in view all along the way—and the views are striking! The Sandy River, fairly shallow and often narrow, above and below the falls, takes on quite a different character in this steep stretch, as the waters pool, twist, swirl, tumble—and roar. Quite a show!

I pick a perch, have a seat, watch and listen, much as I do when at, say Pemaquid Point, or at West Quoddy Head, on the coast of Maine. The great rise and fall, sway and crash of waters—draws people wherever wild waters pulse and sing. Smalls Falls is one of those places!

Chandler Mill Stream Falls

Maine Public Reserved Land
Letter E Plantation

Overview: Adjacent to Smalls Falls (above). 0.2 mile one-way ascent (0.4 miles round-trip) of a hillside to reach overlooks of a dramatic, deep gorge with a series of high falls and deep pools. Often referred to as "The Other Smalls Falls", Chandler Mill Stream Falls is a curiosity—not marked on any maps, yet well-known to locals. Trail unmarked but well-worn by visitors.

No fencing or guard-rails. Use care with children. Along with a visit to Smalls Falls, spend another half-hour or more exploring the viewpoints along Chandler Mill Stream. The falls at high water are dramatic indeed!

Trailhead: Same as for Smalls Falls (above). West side Maine Highway 4 in Letter E Plantation, north of Madrid; south of Rangeley. Prominently signed. Drive in 0.1 mile on signed driveway to parking and picnic area. Trail starts at north end of parking area where a footbridge crosses the Sandy River.

From the end of the Smalls Falls footbridge go straight ahead, past a sign indicating that the area beyond the sign is being kept in a natural condition (i.e. no marked trail)—and up the hill. A number of worn routes lead over rock outcrops under high pines and hemlock to the first overlooks of the falls. Continue upstream for more (dramatic) overlooks.

Nearest Towns: Rangeley (north); Phillips (south)

Maps: Delorme *Maine Atlas* Map #19, 1-A. As above, look for Smalls Falls Rest Area on Maine Highway Maps. USGS: Jackson Mountain

Elevation Gain: 200′ to upper falls.

On Trail:

After crossing the foot bridge over the Sandy River at the base of Smalls Falls, head straight up the hill beyond the bridge. In the first 200 feet the way rises steadily—but the grade will ease. In five minutes or so I hear the rush of the stream. I step around a small knob—and behold!

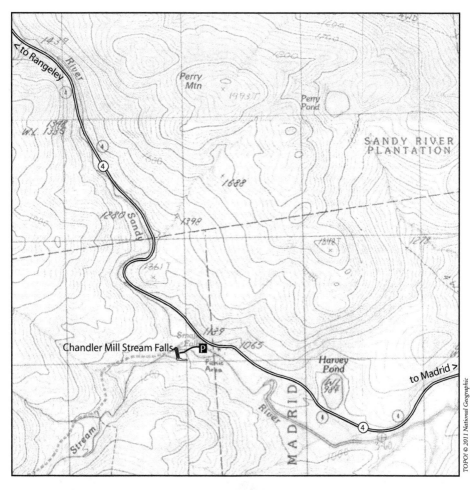

Hidden in plain sight, minutes from popular Smalls Falls, roaring falls tumble 30′ into a sharply cut gorge. I angle my way along the rim of the gorge, seeking different perspectives, watch the high waters fall into ledge-lined pools below. More falls await upstream. I hike on, to yet another set of falls—and another. Dramatic as these falls are, I have the scene all to myself, even as the parking lot for Smalls Falls has many a vehicle. On other days when I have come here, I often meet one or two others hiking up the hill, but rarely more than that. Personal waterfalls anyone?

I complete my hike by the top of the upper falls. The shading woods nearby offer silent beauty, the only sound the clatter and rush of the stream far below. High hemlock rise above the needle-strewn forest floor. Such a peaceful place— and no more than 0.2 mile above the footbridge.

Chandler Mills Falls

FIELD NOTES

Angel Falls

Township D, South of Rangeley and Oquossoc

Overview: 90' high waterfall on Mountain Brook that gains its name from the falling, fanning, waters that at mid to high water levels display the shape of a side-on view of an angel with wings. 0.8 mile hike (1.6 miles round-trip) over rising ground, with stream crossings by foot (no footbridges)—rock stepping at low water, fording at high water. Footwear with good grip and trekking poles/walking staff are advised for stability in crossing the brook, as crossings are over rocks that can be slippery.

Popular with Rangeley Region visitors even though it is a 40 minute drive south of Oquossoc. (See Weld-Mt. Blue section of this book for directions from Weld area.)

Trailhead: From downtown Rangeley, drive west on Maine Highway 4 to Oquossoc and Maine Highway 17 south (towards Byron and Mexico). Drive south on Highway 17 for 18 miles and turn right on the Bemis Road (known locally as Bemis Track, as it is the former Bemis railroad route).

Pass the tiny settlement of Houghton (2–3 camps). Look for a green "Houghton" sign high above the roadway, on left. From Highway 17, drive 3.7 miles north on the Bemis Road. Watch for a sign for Angel Falls parking on the left. Park here or continue on the side road immediately beyond on left. This side road drops down into the valley of Berdeen Stream to a second parking area, where the red-blazed trail begins.

The red-blazed trail heads south over fairly level ground, crossing a former log-landing area, and eventually Berdeen Stream, before swing more westerly to ascend to the falls.

Maps: Delorme *Maine Atlas* Map #18, 4-B, 5-B; USGS: Houghton

Elevation gain: 500'

On Trail:

I choose a fall morning, mid-week, for a hike to Angel Falls. Sugar maple leaves of red and orange flutter on the wind, along with the yellows of popple (as-

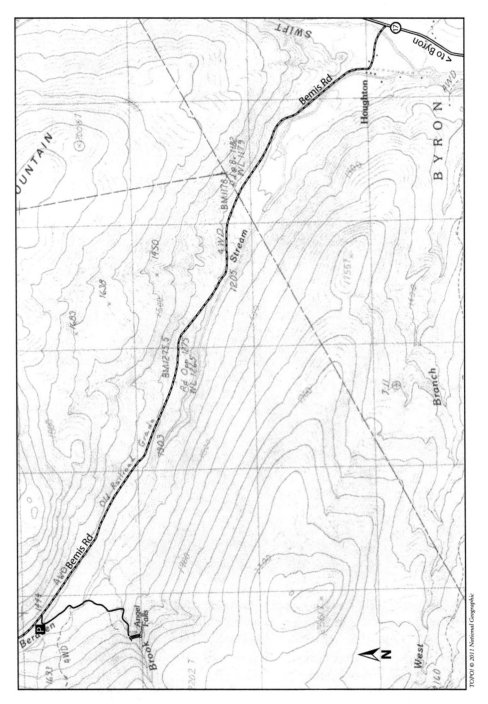

pen) and white birch. Sumac flames red. The cool air is sweetness following the heavy dew of the night before.

My parking choice is the upper parking area on the Bemis Road, for no other reason than a desire to have as much of a walk as I might. There are no other vehicles in sight, although other visitors arrive in the course of my outing. I walk west down the 0.1 mile curving driveway to the larger parking area, which has a great glacial erratic boulder plunked nearly center stage. Although the product of glacial movement, the position suggests that when the parking area was landscaped following logging operations, it was earth-moving equipment rather than a glacier itself, that placed the boulder where it now rests.

The trailhead with its red markings departs at the south edge of the parking area. At first I walk through the essentially level area of a former log-landing—i.e. the area where tree-length wood is hauled out of the forest to be sorted, cut to length as necessary, and loaded onto logging trucks. The trail crosses south-east-flowing Berdeen Stream, quite shallow on this late season day, such that I rock step across—no wet feet here. As usual, I hike with trekking poles—always handy when stepping-rock-to-rock at stream crossings.

The trail swings left after the crossing, winding upward to reach northeast-flowing Mountain Brook above Berdeen Stream. From this point on, the trail runs to the brook. Mountain Brook is also at a low-water flow but the crossings here require concentration, particularly where the brook passes over sloping ledge and there is wet moss at the meeting of water and rock. No quick movements here. I make certain that I have a good foot grip on the rock at each step, and plant my trekking poles firmly, as I make my way across.

A low roar announces the falls, which appear around a final corner—all the better this way, for they come as a visual surprise, like a discovery! I enjoy the moment of surprise!

Although the water is at a moderate level, the water tumble is mighty impressive! A high rock wall rises against the hillside. Through a gap at the top of the falls Mountain Brook pours onto a great, dark rock face, broken by a series of outcrops into a half-dozen separate flowings, fanning out into an angel-wing shape, before dropping into a lower curtain of waters rejoined. I work my way around the base rocks, angling for different views, as the incessant roar and tumble carry on.

Time for lunch. I break out my PB&J sandwich, and an apple; sit, watch, listen. I am struck by how waterfalls continually change flow and shape, moment to moment. What accounts for the uneven flows that vary for a few seconds? I both know and don't know. Water collects in a tiny depression or crack in the rock, fills a miniature pool, spills over, fills again. Something like watching a painting as it is being painted, coming into being before my very eyes. I sit a similar watch on the Maine Coast, as incoming breakers rise and fall, splash and withdraw, each a bit different from the one before, the overall image a constant.

The changing colors of the hardwoods on either side of the falls frame the scene. A good day to be in the Maine woods! On the way out I meet a carload of visitors from Virginia, down from Rangeley for a walk to the falls. I wish them a good fall day.

Visit throughout the hiking season. Spring will bring high water, and quite a display as waters roar over the 90′ drop. At mid-summer the waters of Berdeen Stream and Mountain Brook may be refreshingly brisk. Fall offers cool days and the bright foliage for which Maine is famous!

Hatchery Brook

Rangeley Lakes Heritage Trust
Rangeley

Overview: One mile (1.0 mile) loop hike with short side trails (0.1 mile or much less) to the three lakeside picnic points on lower City Cove on Rangeley Lake, each with a picnic site: "Heron", "Mallard", and "Loon". Little to no elevation gain. Trail passes through mixed hardwood-softwood forest and over bridged bogs. Views of the east shore of Rangeley Lake, and of the peaks of the Saddleback Range. Good choice for a lakeside lunch, or for a short walk to water. An evening walk would offer lowering sun lighting up the heights of Saddleback Mountain, The Horn, and Saddleback Junior. On a rainy day the trail offers a fine sampling of Maine trees, wildflowers, ferns, and mosses, for identification.

Trailhead: Manor Road, off Maine Highway 4, 0.5 mile west of "Moose Alley" at western edge of downtown Rangeley. From Rangeley, make a left turn, across from the cemetery on right. From Oquossuc, on Highway 4, when descending the long hill immediately west of Rangeley, with the downtown area coming into view, the Manor Road is a right turn at the bottom of the hill. Rangeley Lakes Heritage Trust sign for Hatchery Brook Preserve. Drive 0.1 mile on Manor Road. Parking area on left. Information kiosk with trail maps.

Nearest Town: Rangeley

Maps: Delorme *Maine Atlas* Map #29, 5-E; Rangeley Lakes Heritage Trust Hatchery Brook Cove Preserve Trails (www.rlht.org); USGS: Rangeley

Elevation gain: Negligible

On Trail:

Seeking a quiet lunch spot, my wife and I explore Hatchery Brook Preserve Trails on an August mid-day. The day has been heating up. Lunch in shoreline shade, cooled by lake breezes, sounds good! At the trail information kiosk we descend 3 landscape tie steps, enter the woods, and immediately come to the loop trail. We opt for the clockwise direction—and off we go.

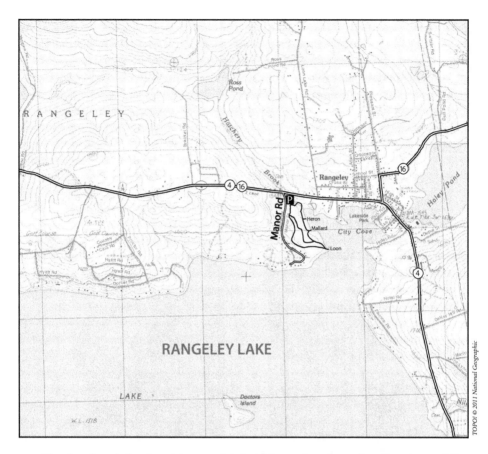

RANGELEY LAKE

TOPO! © 2011 National Geographic

The level path leads past a patch of goldenrod and raspberries. As we hike in the shade of forest canopy, ferns, bunchberry, and sphagnum moss line the route. Spruce, fir, cedar, paper birch, rock maple and a few white maple, populate the forest. Road noise quickly fades as we move into the woods. In a quarter mile we come to the first lakeside site, "Heron" with a picnic table. We continue southward past "Mallard" picnic site, to make "Loon", farthest lake-ward of the sites, our destination.

White paint blazes mark the trail, and each picnic point has a sign. Between Mallard and Loon the MCC Trail enters from the right. This route offers a shortcut back to the parking lot. For particularly wet times of the year the MCC Trail provides a drier pathway than the main trail which, after Loon, crosses 3 bogs— on bog bridges that may be at water level at spring run-off or after heavy rains.

At Loon site, we have a seat at the table, break out lunch, enjoy the lake breeze, and have a look at the Saddleback Range rising above Dallas Hill past the east end of Rangeley Lake. There are people on shore across the cove, but we hear little of their voices. What we *do* hear is a family of Canada geese off a point across from ours. They feed and preen, and otherwise go about their geese business. I spy the flap of a dark wing, plunge of a bill into water, highlighted in midday sun. Then there is the occasional parent-to-child squawk.

We rise to complete our loop hike. Keeping to the outer perimeter, we continue in a clockwise direction. A planked bridge, then cedar slab bridges, keep us above the water. These forest wetlands are precious ecosystems, providing nutrients for fish populations, and feeding grounds for moose, deer, and other creatures.

The upper end of the MCC Trail enters from the right. We cross one more bog bridge, walk another 0.2 mile to reach the junction where we began our loop trail hike. A left on the short spur brings us to the parking lot. Our walk, with a long lunch stop, has taken about one hour.

Walk it in a half-hour, linger over lunch. Come for the birdlife either side of dawn. Hike here for the alpenglow on the mountains at the end of the day. Settle at one of the lakeside lookout points. Enjoy!

For information on Rangeley Lakes Heritage Trust, its conserved lands and trails, go to www.rlht or, or call 207–864–7311.

Mingo Springs Birding Trail
Rangeley

Overview: Two well-designed walking, birding, and nature trails on a north hillside above Rangeley Lake, the Red Trail and the Blue Trail, pass through level to rolling forest, and over open fields with long views. Saddleback and Redington Ranges, and Mt. Abraham rise to the east. Spotted Mountain and the East Kennebago Range rise to the north.

Combined total distance of the two trails 3.0 miles. Shorter walks available by hiking the 2.0 mile Red Trail only; or the 1.0 mile Blue Trail only. Add 0.4 mile if hiking only one of the trails in order to return to the trailhead and parking area along the Mingo Loop Road (i.e., Red Trail, 2.0 + 0.4 = 2.4 miles; Blue Trail, 1.0 + 0.4 = 1.4 miles.)

Both trails lie on land of the Mingo Springs Golf Course, but are out of sight of the course itself over much of their length. Trails are open all year—available for snowshoe travel in winter. Birding brochures, a fern identification flyer, and trail maps available at trailhead kiosk and/or at the nearby Pro Shop from spring through early fall. Signs along the route identify over a dozen different hardwood and softwood trees, and a dozen different ferns.

Course design by John Bicknell, head of Groundskeeping for Mingo Springs Golf Course. Interpretative signs and brochures developed by Maine Master Naturalist Nini Christensen. Photographs by Nick Leadley of *Touch the Wild* photography.

Trailhead: The trailhead and kiosk for the both Red Trail and Blue Trails is on the Mingo Loop Road, across from the intersection with Alpine Way. Mingo Loop Road connects with Maine Highways 4 and 16 west of Rangeley at two junctions: 2.2 miles west of downtown Rangeley, and 0.7 east of Oquossoc. Of the two, the one closer to Rangeley is the more direct approach. (Delorme *Maine Atlas* Map #28, 4-E)

On Mingo Loop (east end) at 0.5 from Highways 4 and 16, look for a prominent green "Mingo Springs Trail" sign on the right, and the intersection with Alpine Way on the left. Park off Alpine Way beside the equipment shed on the golf course side of the road. Sign: "Trail Parking"

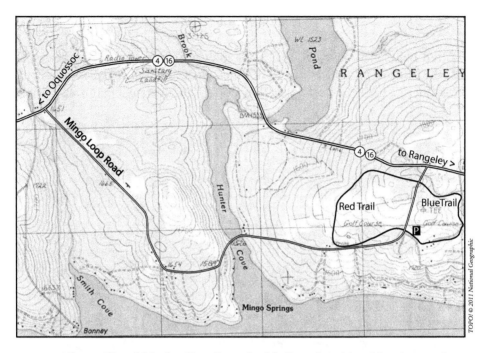

The trailhead kiosk offers flyers for birding, fern identification, and trail layout. If there are none left, copies may be available in season at the Pro Shop, up the hill on Country Club Drive, on the left—which is on the Blue Trail.

The Red Trail enters the woods beyond the trail kiosk, arcs 2.0 miles west, north, and then east, to rejoin the Mingo Loop Road 0.4 miles from the trailhead and parking area. Here hikers may walk back to the trailhead, southward, along the road. Alternately, hikers may cross the road leaving the Red Trail to enter the Blue Trail. The Blue Trail runs 1.0 mile east, south, then west, to arrive back at the trailhead and parking area.

Both trails are well-marked by paint blazes and wooden directional arrows.

Nearest Towns: Rangeley, Oquossoc

Maps: Delorme *Maine Atlas* Map #28, 4-E; Trail maps on site; master map displayed on trailhead kiosk; in season, maps available at golf course Pro Shop in season; USGS: Rangeley

Elevation Gain: ca. 50′ on each trail.

On Trail:

Trail building is alive and well in Franklin County! One of the newest is the Mingo Springs Birding Trail, which circles the upper region of a high, view-offering hill 2.0 miles west of downtown Rangeley, passing through classic

Maine mixed softwood-hardwood forest, skirting small bogs, and opening to see-forever views of Maine's High Peaks.

The well-constructed trail is actually two trails in one—the 2.4 mile Red Trail; and the 1.4 mile Blue Trail, which link to form a 3.0 mile total loop. Many minds and hands have come together on this: John Bicknell, head of grounds keeping at Mingo Springs Golf Club, designed the trail and has overseen its construction by the Mingo Springs grounds crew. Naturalist Kirk Betts and naturalist-photographer Nick Leadley surveyed the bird populations in order to make the trail into Maine's newest Birding Trail. Naturalist Nini Chistensen took on the tasks of tree and fern identification, and the installation of interpretive signs along the trail. Underwriting the costs of constructing the trail is the Chodosh family. A true community effort!

On a June visit, the most recent of many hikes there, my wife and I walk both the Red Trail and Blue Trail on a bright and breezy, late afternoon. It is a warm day, and we welcome the coolness of the shaded woods we enter on the Red Trail. Well-used to the rocks and roots of many a Maine trail, instead, here we enjoy a graded footpath, 4–5 feet wide. Rock maple rise here, as do "popple", the local term for aspen. A tiny vernal pool lies in a small bog to our right. Ferns abound in a small meadow beyond the bog. Wild blueberry bushes line the trail—berries will arrive in a few weeks!

The forest soon becomes more mixed: balsam fir, beech, red maple, a rock maple 18″ in diameter, and an even broader white ash 2′ or more across at a point 4′ off the ground. Signs placed in this section, and beyond, along both trails, identify a specimen of each tree species to be found on the trail system. A massive yellow birch stands with a 2′ diameter. The high forest canopy shields the forest floor from much of the sun. As a result there is little undergrowth in this section. Soft light making a way through the leaves falls on ages of accumulated rusty brown leaf drop.

The Red Trail ascends a short rise, descends to cross a low area by a boardwalk, and reaches the western extension of Mingo Road. We follow the road northward 0.2 mile with the golf course on the right, rimmed by a stand of great-girthed white birch, high tops waving in the afternoon wind. The rich deep blue of Rangeley Lake appears through a break in the trees to our left. After passing a white farm house which stands to our right, the Red Trail turns 90 degrees to the right, and we re-enter the woods. Another boardwalk crosses a small boggy area, and the Red Trail ascends gradually through mixed hardwood-softwood growth for the next 1.0 mile.

Although the trail circles the golf course, over most of the distance the course is well out-of-sight. We could just as well be deep in the Maine woods, far from any town, flanked as we are by high pine, great rock maple, white and brown ash, yellow birch, beech, hemlock, fir, spruce—and even tamarack (aka larch or hackmatack), the only Maine conifer to turn bright amber in the fall, then drop all of its needles.

The drumming of a woodpecker gets our attention. We sit on a convenient cedar bench, hold quiet, and listen. The drummer? A yellow-bellied sapsucker. Through binoculars (Do bring binoculars!) we watch this industrious bird drill away on a white birch, making another in a line of holes to which it will return to draw out birch sap.

Two miles of hiking has taken us just under an hour, with stops to look and listen for birds, when we reach the Mingo Springs Loop Road. We could head back along the road for 0.4 miles to reach the trailhead and our vehicle—or cross the road where there is an entrance to the Blue Trail. No question—we want more! On to the Blue Trail!

More quiet forest, more well-graded trail—even a low section where trail builders have hauled in rock to line the trail, filling the low area with gravel and wood chips.

We ascend a small hill, slabbing to the south side, to emerge at the edge of a hay field. The Saddleback Range appears in the distance as we cross the field, re-enter the woods, emerge once again into a broad field of lupine, blues and pinks, covering the east-facing slope of the hill below the golf course. On this breezy and bright June day we walk through a sea of sun-lit lupine. Quite a sight!

Bring on the views! In the east rise Maine's High Peaks: the long north-south ridge of Mt. Abraham (Abram to locals); Spaulding; Sugarloaf; and through a gap in the ranges, the near-twin Bigelow Range peaks of West Peak and Avery. Closer in the east rise the Crockers, North and South, and the Redington Range. As the trail rises now, gaining the high ground, we have a view to the north towards Spotted Mountain and the East Kennebago Range. Following our hike I check the elevation. Our high point on this level to gently rolling terrain is 1800′—and to reach that we have gained not more than 100′ of elevation on this thoughtfully constructed course. Not a bad view for that amount of effort!

The final 0.3 miles of the Blue Trail parallels the access road for the Golf Club, passing the Pro Shop. That view of the High Peaks, now behind us, draws us time and time again to turn around for yet another look. A short descent and we are back at the parking area and trailhead. A good hike!

Mingo Springs Birding Trail has already hosted an Audubon Walk, and the trail is now holds Audubon Certification—one of three birding trails in Maine to have that honor.

Many hiking options! Walk one trail or both. Hike in either direction! Do a figure eight! Choose this route for a rainy day hike. Come back in winter to hike the route on snowshoes, and count the winter birds—blue jays, chickadees, and all the rest. See it in all its moods and seasons.

The trail is open all year.

Bonney Point

Rangeley Lakes Heritage Trust
Rangeley

Overview: 1 mile loop, additional 0.2 mile spur leading to Smith Cove, north shore of Rangeley Lake. Gradual descent toward the lake; ascent on return. Forest trail over once-sheep pasture on side hill above the lake, leading to views from the shore southward across the lake towards Four Ponds Mountain and Beaver Mountain, and the terrain of Rangeley Lake State Park. Picnic table at cove.

Trailhead: 0.5 miles on Bonney Point Road, from Maine Highway 16, west of the downtown Rangeley junction of Highways 4 and 16. Watch for the sign on Highway 16: *Bonney Point Conservation Lands—Rangeley Lakes Heritage Trust.* The parking area and trail kiosk are in a small meadow on the left side of the road. A single path leads into the woods, then divides north-south for the two arms of the loop trail. The clockwise arm of these trails is slightly longer at 0.6 mile and the counter-clockwise arm is 0.4 miles.

The two rejoin at the spur trail to Smith Cove at the southern extreme of both sections of the loop. The north arm is marked with white blazes; the south arm and spur trail are marked with yellow blazes.

Nearest Town: Rangeley

Maps: Delorme *Maine Atlas* Map #28, 4-E; Bonney Point Map, Rangeley Lakes Heritage Trust;

USGS: Rangeley

Elevation Gain: 200′

On Trail:

Decisions, decisions: Hike clockwise? Counterclockwise? One August day I choose clockwise. The map at the Bonney Point Trailhead kiosk depicts the first as slightly longer than the second. My plan is to cover the full loop anyway, but on some matter of principle—take the long way in, the shorter out, I opt as I

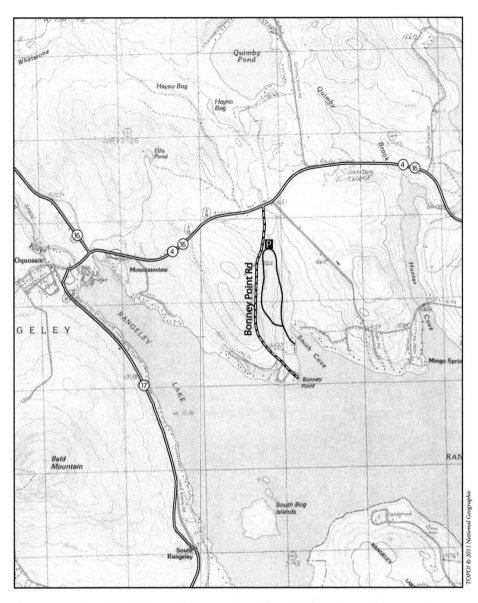

do. I pass a few white birch, quickly enter a forest where balsam fir predominates, heading north, and soon arcing east and then south.

The trail slabs across a hillside that once served as sheep pasture. This hill, in fact, was historically known as Sheep's Hill. When sheep farming declined, the land reverted to forest. Still, it is good to imagine the day when the thick woods above the north shore of Rangeley Lake was once working agricultural land, and was a source of woolen goods for the region and for the nation.

I pass old routes that cross the trail, some the vestiges of farm roads, others surely twitch trails from logging operations; and small meadows. It is goldenrod season, and these leggy yellow-topped flowers are frequent along the way. Buttercups populate the open areas, and ferns are thick in the shade.

After 15 minutes of what has been mostly descent, I reach the spur trail to the lake, and turn left, which is south. The trail makes a jog to the north before ending at Smith Cove. A picnic table stands on the lakeside shore of the cove, with good views southward across Rangeley Lake. That view takes in the long ridge south of the lake that divides the valley of Rangeley Lake from the Sandy River and Swift River drainages on the other side of the ridge. Beaver Mountain, 3160′ in elevation, tops the eastern end of that high ground, and Four Ponds

Mountain, 2910′ is the high point toward the western end. I enjoy the long view from a shady spot by the shore.

Hikers who choose early morning or evening to be on this trail may see wildlife at the inlet to Smith Cove. Watch for beaver who have constructed a lodge near that inlet. I have been here when there are loons in the cove, as power boats tend not to venture here. Loons build their nests very close to the water, and these nests are vulnerable to waves from powerboat wakes—even small waves. At high summer, when the outer lake is at its busiest with boaters, Smith Cove usually remains a quite, place-apart, spot.

Occasionally paddlers on the Northern Forest Canoe Trail pull in to Smith Cove for a lunch break. No one is here on this day, but what a bonus it would be to meet people who are on that 742 mile route from Old Forge, New York, to Fort Kent, Maine. I have spoken with such paddlers at other points along that route. Each has many a good story to tell.

On my return hike, when I hike the spur trail to the loop trail, I turn left to complete the remaining 0.4 miles of the full loop. Up the hill to the meadow where the trail divides—imagining the day when sheepherders worked their flocks on this now-forested hillside.

Bonney Point offers the only trail access of its kind along the north shore—a midpoint along the shore, away from town, a bit of up and down. How about a short walk to water in summer! Or hike here to watch the forest and shore come alive in spring. Watch the fall colors emerge from this pristine lakeside vantage point. If giving thought to stepping into the water, river sandals or another type of water footwear are a good idea here—as in most Maine inland waters, the lake bottom may vary from sand to cobble to mud or tree-tumbled twigs and branches brought down by the wind and snow.

Hunter Cove

Rangeley Lakes Heritage Trust
Rangeley

Overview: 1.0 mile hiking loop over level, variably-forested terrain and bog crossed by bog bridges reaching upper region of sheltered Hunter Cove on north side of Rangeley Lake. Good for a short morning walk, a lunch hike, or an evening hike to the west-facing shore for the last light of day. Three short cross-trails cut across the loop route, providing options to extend—or shorten—the hike.

A good choice on blustery days, as the surrounding woodland offers protection from wind—or hike here on a rainy day for exercise and nature study. The route passes through stands of Norway spruce, and of white pine; marshland alder thickets; hardwood stands of maple, beech, and birch; and cove-side cedar. Bring a wildflower book!

Trailhead: 3.0 mile west of Downtown Rangeley, off south side of Maine Highway 16 (sign). Parking area with privy and trail kiosk.

Note: This area is *not* Hunter Cove Uplands, which are lands to the west of this trailhead. Hunter Cove *Conservation Area Trails* and Hunter Cove *Uplands* are two different locales. Trails described below lead from the well-signed parking area, up a short hill from Highway 16, as indicated above.

The Red Trail is a loop that begins at the parking area, extends to the east shore of Hunter Cove, and returns. Three short trails: Green, Blue, Yellow, cut across the loop at various points—as indicated on the map at the trailhead kiosk. All four trails cross some combination of forest and bog footpath. The Red Trail has more wooded pathway. The three shorter trails include more bog terrain. The opportunity to see varied wildlife and plant life increases with the variety of terrain.

The Red Trail loop arm *north*, the shorter route to the cove, leaves from the trail kiosk at a diagonal right. The Red Trail loop arm *south* departs from the southeast (Rangeley Village direction) corner of the parking lot, about 50 feet to the left of the kiosk. The two arms of the loop join at Hunter Cove.

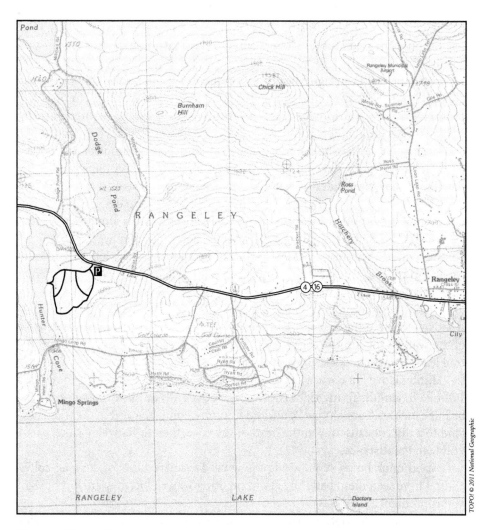

Nearest Town: Rangeley

Maps: Delorme *Maine Atlas* Map #28, 4-E; Hunter Cove Conservation Area
Map, Rangeley Lakes Heritage Trust; USGS: Rangeley.

Elevation Gain: Negligible.

On Trail:

Many a time I have driven past the sign for Hunter Cove Sanctuary without stopping, on my way to fly-fish in the waters west of Rangeley, or for mountain peak hikes. On one particular sun-filled day, after a high country hike of a few hours, I decided to stop. It is good to stretch the legs after a long hike, but I soon learn that Hunter Cove is surely a destination in its own right—well worth its own visit.

From the trailhead sign I head west on the Red Trail, marked by metal discs attached to trees, passing through well-shaded forest that is curious for its stand of Norway spruce. Curious, because this spruce is not native to Maine. Those familiar with the six conifers common to Maine—pine, spruce, fir, hemlock, cedar, and larch—will notice the difference. Norway spruce, for example, have reddish bark, unlike the scaly bark of black spruce or red spruce; and their needles are flat, like fir, not three-sided as is usually distinctive for spruce.

These trees, native to Europe, were introduced a few decades ago, by a previous landowner. Another location where I have seen them is along the Fly Rod Crosby Trail, 0.3 miles north of Reeds Mill. There, too, they were introduced. You won't find them in most Maine tree books, so bring along a book of North American trees to study them and regard their particular appearance, different from the neighboring growth.

I pass these conifers to enter a mixed growth area—hardwoods and softwoods— to reach the east shore of Hunter Cove. A short spur leads to the edge of the water. One hundred feet beyond, along the trail, another opening to the trail leads to a small dock. Choose your spot!

Hunter Cove is a narrow, rectangular arm of Rangeley Lake, a bit more than 1.0 mile in length. To my right (north), the cove ends at its northern reach, fed by inlet streams from Dodge Pond, and Quimby Pond. To my left, the waters extend to a distant causeway at the head of the cove, then to Rangeley Lake, partly visible in the distance.

Wood duck boxes stand along the cove. These are birds of striking coloration. I have seen them paddling about on other waters, but they are out of sight at this moment.

As the day enters late afternoon, the cove waters lie still, mirroring cove-side growth of cedar, fir, and red maple. I step out onto a small dock that offers a vantage point. Out by the lake there are homes and camps, but these are hidden from view. A vehicle crosses the far-off causeway, but I hear no sound. For now Hunter Cove is a world apart.

From the dock I re-enter the woods on the Red Trail, continue the loop hike in a counter-clockwise direction, and on the way eastward pass intersections for the Yellow, Blue, and Green trails, which cut across the great circle formed by the Red Trail. Much variety here—alders in wetlands skirted by the trail, red maples, fir, and pine. Chickadees sing as evening comes on.

I reach the end of the Red Trail at the east end of the parking area, about 50 feet from the trail kiosk at the west end of the lot. Hikers who plan to hike clockwise should note this. If at the trail kiosk and wishing to take the Red Trail east before turning south and west, walk back into the parking area to locate the red medallions that mark the Red Trail.

Since my first hike I have returned to hike all of the colored trails. Distances are short, discoveries aplenty. Start the day here, end it here, or bring a lunch to enjoy at the water's edge!

Rangeley River Trail

Rangeley Lakes Heritage Trust
Oquossoc

Overview: One mile one-way (2.0 miles round-trip) trail connecting Rangeley River area near Maine Highway 16 north of Oquossoc with Oquossoc Village, crossing Rangeley River by a snowmobile bridge, and offering a 0.3 spur to a cove on Mooselookmeguntic Lake. Part of the route is a portage path for the Northern Forest Canoe Trail, hence the 0.3 mile side trail to a dry-ki cove on the lake, not far from so-called Indian Rock and the outlet of Rangeley River to the lake. Picnic tables on both sides of Rangeley River crossing. Portions of the route were once rail bed for a logging railroad accessing Kennebago Lake, and, accordingly, are straight and level.

Sheltered from wind and well-shaded. Good choice for a hot day or rainy day walk. Variety of ecological niches, including river, lake shore and marsh, hardwoods and conifers, provide opportunities to view moose, birds, and other wildlife.

Trailheads: *North.* From junction of Maine Highways 4 and 16 east of Oquossoc Village, drive north on Highway 16 for 1.0 mile to an angled side road on the left (west) side. Rangeley Lakes Heritage Trust sign. Follow this gravel road 0.2 miles, keeping to the left to pass three side roads, to reach a parking area by a metal gate. On the other side of the gate is an RLHT sign.

South: Park in a public space in vicinity of Oquossoc General Store. Between the store and Oquossoc Marine, walk on the Hatchery Road 0.1 mile to a Y-intersection. Hatchery Road veers slightly right. The Rangeley River Trail bears *left*, meeting a metal gate in under 100'. Snowmobile trail sign for ITS 84. Trail kiosk beyond the gate on left.

Nearest town: Oquossoc

Maps: Delorme *Maine Atlas* Map #28, 3-E; USGS: Oquossoc

Elevation gain: Minimal, less than 50 feet.

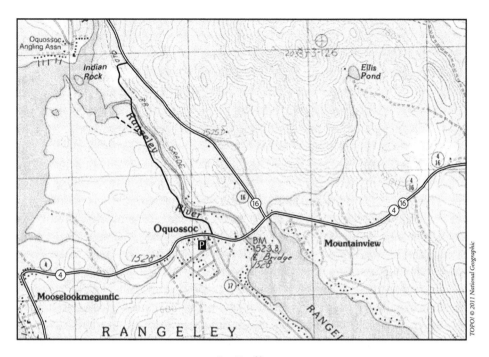

TOPO! © 2011 National Geographic

On Trail:

As I approach the south trailhead from Oquossoc Village, a yearling moose steps from the woods to my left, cuts in front of me with barely a side glance, trots down the trail. The awkward-looking, but deftly moving moose, making a quick move around the steel gate that marks the south end of the trail, trots down the trail. Never know when a moose will appear! I am only 50' from the gate when it passes me, but by the time I reach the gate and have a clear view down the straight-as-an-arrow trail, the fluid trot of that young moose has brought it far down the path. One more glimpse: a brown-black hind end disappears into the distance. That was a treat.

It is a sunny day, veering towards hot out in the village. Here I enjoy the shade of a green tunnel, bordered by a mix of balsam fir, red maple, and white birch. Bunchberry with their creamy-yellow flowers line the woods on either side of the trail. In less than a month they will produce the tightly bunched red berries that give this common Maine woods wildflower its name.

In 0.5 mile from the gate, the main trail swings to the right, while a spur—serving as a portage trail between Mooselookmeguntic and Rangeley Lakes—angles left. I choose the spur, which makes a slight S-turn and descends to the water. No bathing beach here! This is a dry-ki cove, a spot where the prevailing northwest winds drive driftwood—known in the north country as "dry-ki"—to the shoreline, where it accumulates. Over the years the wood will deteriorate and become part of the marshy shoreline. For now, the dry-ki would make this a tough spot from which to pull a canoe from the water, unless a paddler was wearing the sturdiest of footwear.

In the distance, at mid-water near the mouth of the cove, stands so-called Indian Rock. In an earlier era this outcrop would have alerted paddlers on Cupsuptic or Mooselookmeguntic Lake that this cove marks the inlet of the Kennebago River and a portage route to Rangeley Lake. (In the present day the two lakes are a continuous body of water, but before the building of Upper Dam in the southwest corner of Mooselookmeguntic Lake, they were separate, linked by a thoroughfare.

The good news is that this sheltered cove, with its marsh and driftwood, makes a good home for waterfowl. A female mallard feeds in gaps among the dry-ki, which provides a windbreak from the prevailing norhwesterlies. I keep silence and remain utterly still, for she has her back to me, and seems not to have noticed my intrusion into her feeding sanctuary.

The mallard feeds, spotting something worth eating, dips her bill to snag it, takes in a bit of water to wash it down, shakes her head from side to side as though to clear whatever water clings to her intricately-patterned brownish head, scans 180 degrees, hops over a 4″ weathered grey plank that once may have been part of the porch floor of a fishing camp, miles upstream. Back to feeding. Dad must be on the nest, elsewhere in this cove, while she feeds, gathering her energy for her turn.

I have written on other occasions what a gift it is to be among creatures in the wild as they feed, or preen, or look after their young, going about their business. They act as they do when humans are not around. This is rare. I am grateful for these moments. Such occasions require silence on my part—and not just silence, but stillness, and deep patience. A whisper to another in a party, a shift in footing—and the creature, alerted, usually bolts. So it is that I stand stock-still, watch, listen to the slight sounds as she raises her bill and water droplets fall into the dark water. Such a time!

A Northern Forest Canoe Trail portage marker is attached to a tree near the water's edge. I doubt that many voyageurs choose this dry-ki route. Most take out at Haines Landing lower on the lake, and walk the Carry Road through Oquossoc Village to reach Rangeley lake.

In the distance, past Indian Rock, lie buildings of the Oquossoc Angling Association, which formed in 1870 to promote fly fishing, drawing anglers from throughout the nation, and beyond, to this hitherto little known fishing region. That history is intriguing, and worth looking up. I am a regular visitor to the Outdoor Heritage Sporting Museum in Oquossoc Village, where there are outstanding displays of the rich history of Rangeley Region fishing.

Back on trail, I pass star flowers and lily of the valley as I hike the 0.3 miles back to the spur trail intersection. Here I turn left to continue north on the main trail, dropping down to another long level stretch. What's that sound? From well off to my right I hear the rattle and rush of the Rangeley River—then catch a glimpse through the cedar and fir of flowing dark blue and white. I am getting close!

At 0.3 mile from the junction I arrive at the bridge. A picnic table sits to the left, by a worn path that leads along the bank, downstream. I step onto the bridge, watch the rapid flow. Two days of rain preceded today's sunny weather. The river flows fairly full and quite quick.

On the far side of the bridge rests another picnic table, a bit worn, and beyond that, the curious sight of a broken-off fir tree that hangs suspended in the embrace of a white birch. I try to reconstruct that story! Past this point a short path off the south side of the trail leads into thicker woods, and a privy. I head straight, ascend a short slope, and arrive at the north gate.

On other days I have started at the north end. Either way I do an out-and-back hike, amounting to an estimated 2 miles. The terrain is quite easy to negotiate, the trail essentially level. What I treasure about this trail is its invitation to keep silence, to watch, to listen, awaiting a discovery.

Tim Baker Nature Trail
Rangeley Region Guides and Sportsmen's Association
Oquossoc

Overview: 0.4 mile forest loop, beginning and ending near a small pond on the grounds of the Rangeley Region Guides and Sportsmen's Association clubhouse in Oquossoc. A good introductory walk for children—and a fine choice for anyone of any age wishing to have a short hike through pristine woods. Named for long-time RRGSA volunteer Tim Baker, an advocate for preservation of the outdoor heritage of the Rangeley region, and for public education about the outdoors. The trail was constructed with assistance from AmeriCorps Volunteers in the summer of 2015.

Trailhead: Clubhouse grounds on Old Skiway Road, Oquossoc, 0.3 mile from Carry Road.

From Oquossoc Village drive west on Carry Road 0.1 mile in direction of Haines Landing. Turn left on Old Skiway Road. The clubhouse on the right. Park in the parking area adjacent to the picnic pavilion, and by the pond.

Hike begins under an overhead sign behind (south) the clubhouse (walk around clubhouse to see the trailhead.) Trail guides available at trailhead.

Nearest Town: Oquossoc

Maps: Delorme *Maine Atlas* Map # 28, 3-E. (Old Skiway Road not designated as such on map, but Carry Road is.); Tim Baker Nature Trail Map at trailhead; USGS: Oquossoc

Elevation Gain: 55'

On Trail:

I am always heartened to learn of nature trails and other projects that welcome the public to learn of the creatures of the Maine woods, and the terrain that serves as their home. Within a day or two of hearing about the new Tim Baker Trail, I am on my way to Oquossoc to hike it. My day was a sunny one in late summer, at mid-week.

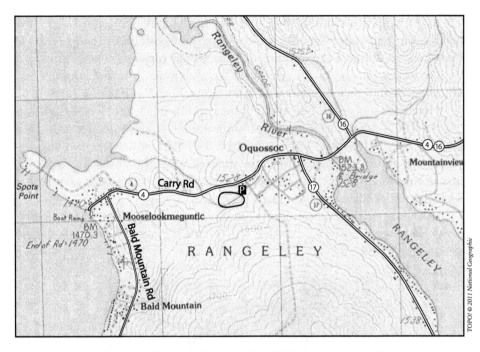

TOPO! © 2011 National Geographic

I enter the blue-marked trail under the high sign, cross a draw by way of a wooden bridge, step into woods where balsam fir predominate, with a few popple (aspen) along the way. The trail ascends a short rise, swinging west, before descending at 0.1 mile to a fern-filled bog, crossed by a bog bridge. Striped maple—known also as "moose maple" for their oversized leaves, grow trailside. Though in the maple family, this tree rarely grows to be more than 4″ in diameter, and seldom reaches more than 20′ high. In fall the leaves turn a bright banana yellow, and the plant may hang on to those leaves a bit longer than does its much large cousins in the maple family.

From the bog the trail ascends once more, on the way to its highest point. I note the fine trail work in this section. Rock placement, gravel fill, and careful grading are thoughtful measures that make the walk a bit easier for hikers, protect against compaction and erosion—and reduce the need for future trail repair.

The next section certainly justifies selection of this route for a nature trail. Tree study anyone? I observe rock (sugar) maple and red maple, white birch and yellow birch, and more striped or moose maple. Two turns, first 90 degrees to the north to begin a descent, with a look at nearby beech and balsam fir; then east 90 degrees. Wildlife? In a small section of mud by the trail—the print of a deer hoof! There is a song in the air—an ovenbird sings "teacher, teacher, teacher!" I pass buttercups, and many, many patches of ferns. (The trail guide identifies four different types of ferns.) Much to see—and hear—on this nature trail.

At 0.3 mile I cross another bog bridge and enter a small meadow with views north toward the hills above Oquossoc. More stonework on the trail here. One more bend to the north, and I encounter balsam fir once again before the final descent to western end of the pond near the clubhouse. It is mid-summer and lupine are in abundance and in full bloom along the grassy bank.

I make my way around the pond to the parking area—a total of 0.4 miles.

My hike did not take long—10–15 minutes including stops. The pond is a good spot to sit for a time—especially early and late in the day when wildlife approach the grassy area that borders the water. If that time-on-trail seems brief, turn around and hike the route once more—in reverse. You may be surprised at what you notice the second time around!

Hike this trail on a sunny day; a rainy day to get outdoors but be in the shelter of the forest; a day when the wind is up on the big lakes, or a day when there are children with you!

Organon Trails
Wilheim Reich Museum
Rangeley

Overview: Main trail is a 1.0 mile loop on the Wilheim Reich Museum 175 acre property known as Organon. Add a 0.2 mile walk (0.4 mile round trip) from the lower parking area to the trailhead behind the museum. Long view over Rangeley lake to the Saddleback Range.

Reich was a psychiatrist and psychoanalyst, and an inventor who studied physics. He sought to discover and use for therapeutic purposes an essential biological force, which he termed "orgone." He purchased the current museum property in 1942, which was a farm at the time, to be a summer home. In 1948 he had the current museum building constructed. Eventually it became a center for his research. Following his death in 1957 at the age of 60, the so-called "Wilheim Reich Infant Trust" formed to establish the property as a museum and educational center.

The Main Trail/Nature Trail route—one of many trails available to the public—leads from the principal museum building west, north, and south, through forest, before entering open fields with southeast views over Rangeley Lake and toward the Saddleback Range. Other trails range from 0.25 miles in the immediate vicinity of Museum building, to 2.2 miles along Quimby Brook. Most trails are forest routes, except for the Main Trail/Nature Trail which at one point crosses the broad open field below the museum, as described herein.

Major hiking attraction is the long view, one of the more readily attainable vantage points in the foothills north of Rangeley Lake—hence its inclusion here. There is an admission fee for the museum, which is open in summer. My hikes have been in early spring or in fall when the buildings were not open. No fee applied to the use of the trail system at that time.

Trailhead: Off Dodge Pond Road, west of Rangeley on Maine Highway 16. Signs on Highway 16, and on Dodge Pond Road, for "Organon." The approach to the property borders an open field that slopes upward to the high ground where the fieldstone museum structure is located.

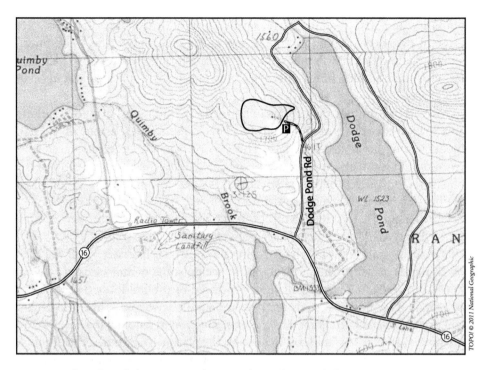

Directional signs on Dodge Pond Road. Turn left at main gate to enter the property. Signs indicate parking area. Off season: park at bottom of hill, near white student center.

Hiking maps on porch of student center. Walk past a seasonal gate uphill to the vicinity of museum. Main hiking trail enters the woods beside bookstore and across the drive from the museum.

Maps: Delorme *Maine Atlas* Map # 28, 4-E (Wilheim Reich Museum designated on map); Organon Trails map available at student center by parking area; USGS: Rangeley

Elevation Gain: ca. 100′

On Trail:

On a fall afternoon my wife and I visit Organon for views we had been told were well worth the hike. We park by the student center, and the gated roadway leading past the center to the museum and bookstore—both of which were closed for the season. Yellow trail maps sit in a box on the student center porch.

The day is partly sunny, and cool—ideal hiking weather. We continue our hikes well into late fall, enjoying the rich light, open forest, air that holds little humidity, and that coolness. Here, on this terrain, leaves have dropped, save those of the beech, adding to the openness. The proximity of field and forest, and Dodge and Quimby Ponds, renders this good birding territory. Maine's winter birds are out and about: chickadee, blue jay, junco. A pileated woodpecker drills away.

We ascend on foot the conifer-lined roadway leading up from the parking area toward the museum and trailhead. This is the steepest ascent of the day, moderated by the roadway surface. This way reaches the large rock-faced museum on the right, and the bookstore on the left. Our hike begins just past the bookstore, on the left beyond a small parking area. This is the so-called Main Trail or Hiking Trail, which leads into the forest, passes the tomb of Wilheim Reich, then arcs to the right to meet the Trail of Thoughts, where signs bearing selected quotations from Reich have been placed along the trail.

We back-track a bit to join the Nature Trail which intersects with the Trail of Thoughts at its north end. Hopeful of seeing some winter birds, we follow the Nature Trail to a large, 8' diameter enclosed bird blind located at the head of a small clearing. Such birds are busy foraging elsewhere at this time of day, and our sightings this day are elsewhere on the property, not by the blind. From the bird blind trail we head southeast over the Nature Trail to descend through mixed softwood-hardwood forest to meet and cross the loop road, and eventually the open, grassy slope below the museum.

Such a view! The great lawn falls away to forest at the foot of the hill. We have a glimpse of Dodge Pond beyond—and beyond that Rangeley Lake, Dallas Hill, and the Saddleback Range. Park benches are located at points along the hill. We sit and look, with no rush whatsoever.

Our 1.4 mile hike, at an easy pace, including the bird blind stop, and the bench stop, has taken about an hour. What are your fall afternoon plans?

Rangeley Lakes Trail Center

Sandy River Plantation

Overview: Forest walks on generally level terrain over Nordic ski and snow-shoe trails situated on the lower north slope of Saddleback Mountain, and south of Saddleback Lake. This entry describes two short and fairly level trails: Tote Road and Lake Trail.

Yurt-style lodge closed outside of winter season, but trails open for public use. Maps available outside the yurt. No fee. Donations welcome.

Good choice for a shaded walk, wildflower or birding walk, or a rainy day hike. Views from cove on Saddleback Lake and from Picnic Point to the Saddleback Range, Potato Nubble, and the Redington Range.

Tote Road Trail, 1.1 miles one-way (2.2 miles round-trip) is abundant with wildflowers in season. At intersection with Lower Pipeline Trail, walk an additional 0.8 mile (1.6 miles round-trip) to shore of Saddleback Lake with views west and north. (Total outing to lake and return: 3.8 miles).

Lake Trail, 0.5 mile (1.0 mile round-trip) descends gradually on a wide and shaded Nordic ski route, white birch-bordered along much of its length, to a lakeside bog and cove beyond, and a picnic table. Watch for birds here, including a bald eagle in the trees to the right (south) of the cove. This Lake Trail hike may be extended another 0.5 miles one-way by hiking to Picnic Point on the west shore of Saddleback Lake, by a foot trail, muddy in spots. If Picnic Point is included, the round-trip from the parking area would be 2.0 miles. Picnic Point has a picnic table. The point offers outstanding views of the Saddleback Range. Total outing to Picnic Point and return: 2.0 miles round trip.

There are many other trails on the grounds of the Trails Center. The above trails are suited for summer use because they are well-traveled and do not require walking through much tall grass or low brush.

Trailhead: 524 Saddleback Mountain Road, Rangeley. From Maine Highway 4, turn east on the Dallas Hill Road across from a prominent highway over-look of Rangeley Lake (Delorme *Maine Atlas* Map 28, 5-E). Follow signs for Saddleback Mountain Ski Area, turning right onto the Saddleback

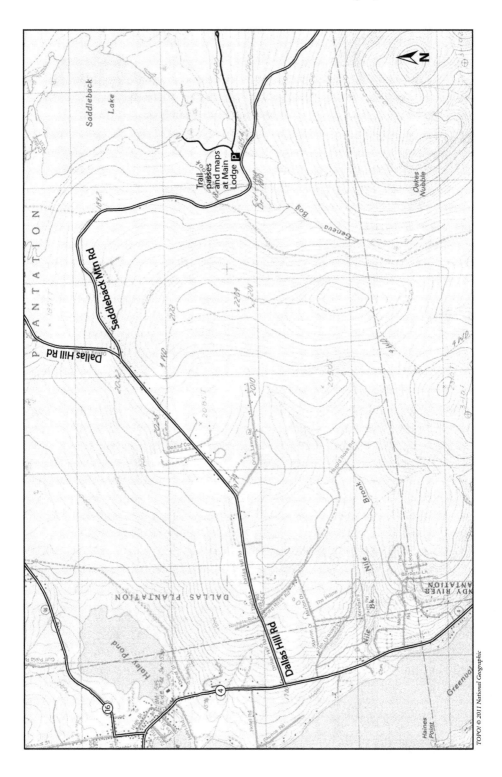

Mountain Road from the Dallas Hill Road. The Rangeley Lakes Trails Center (RLTC) is on the left. Watch for the yurt-style lodge.

The Trails Center system is open all year, but is staffed only in winter and for special events in other seasons. A sign board displays a system map. Paper maps are usually available in a map box.

Nearest Town: Rangeley

Maps: Delorme *Maine Atlas* Map #29, 1-E (Look for area by Geneva Bog Brook); Rangeley Lakes Trail Center Map (on signboard and in paper copies at trailhead); USGS: Saddleback Mountain

Elevation Gain: less than 100'

On Trail:

On a July day of intermittent sun and rain, my wife and I look forward to a walk in the woods with our Chocolate Labrador Retriever "Moose". The Saddleback Range is shrouded in clouds, as are many of the lower peaks in the Rangeley region. We have always enjoyed snowshoeing and skiing at the Rangeley Lakes Trail Center, and decide to head there for a hike. The yurt-style lodge is closed for the season, but the parking lot is open, and a signboard displays the trail system map. Below the board a map box contain paper copies. Although I am familiar with the trails from winter use, I take a map in the event that we opt for a new route, or simply because surroundings appear different in July from the way they look, snow-covered, in February or March.

Tote Road.

We choose Tote Road, a grassy woods road—two tracks with grass in the center. It has a firm base and is quite dry in spite of recent rain. Tote Road runs east for 1.1 mile to a junction with the Pipeline Trails—Upper and Lower. We will decide at this junction whether to take Lower Pipeline down to the east shore of Saddleback Lake, or to return to the lodge to then hike the Lake Trail to the south shore.

Tote Road is a good choice, surprising us with a remarkable display of wild-flowers. Location, location, location! This trail with its east-west orientation, and its width as an old road, has the benefit of sun exposure. North-south trails will have more winter sun; and narrower trails will have more shade, but Tote Road is well-suited for wildflower growth.

Lupine are among the first summer wildflowers, a deep blue-purple, and some reddish-pink. Buttercups and colts foot, bright yellow, abound. So too do purple vetch, paintbrush in its flaming red-orange, and clover, both red and

white. In the course of the hike we also see daisies and brown-eyed Susans. There are others we are unable to identify—should have brought the wildflower book! We photograph these.

Tote Road passes a series of trail junctions marked by diamond-shaped signs with letters coded to the map, but with most of these also labeled with wooden trail signs bearing names like Moose Alley, Anne's Trail, and Pulp Run. We stay with Tote Road, crossing a number of streams by bridges, to reach a 4-way intersection with Upper Pipeline to our right (south); Bridge Trail straight ahead (west); and Lower Pipeline to our left (north).

We could take Lower Pipeline to the lakeshore, but decide instead to retrace our steps and then explore the Lake Trail which leads from the trailhead to the southwest corner of the lake. Back we go, stopping often for wildflower photographs.

Lake Trail.

To reach this trail we walk to the back of the parking lot (south), with the yurt to our left, crossing an open field and descending a short slope to a much larger field. This serves as the "stadium" for winter Nordic ski and snowshoe competitions. Do not expect any bleachers! The only sign that this may be a competition start-finish area is a small wooden building used by race officials.

On the far side of the stadium, look for angled orange signs reading "Snow-shoe Alley". This marks the entrance to the Lake Trail. Cross the grassy stadium to enter the woods. Just past the snowshoe signs a wooden sign reads "Lake Trail". The trail is wide, nearly as wide as Tote Road, and a well-worn footpath leads through the grassy route to descend 0.5 mile to the lake.

The Lake Trail catches much less sun than Tote Road, as it has a north-south orientation and is bordered by high deciduous trees, predominantly white birch, white maple, and sugar maple. The sun breaks through in places to shine on the birch, lending a contrast between the dark forest floor and the bright white bark and pale green canopy of the birch. In place of the great variety of wildflowers on Tote Road, here we see bunchberry in abundance, along with moss, and, where suns does find its way, many stands of fern.

The trail ends at an opening towards the lake, which stands on the far side of a boggy inlet. Across the lake rises cone-shaped Potato Nubble, a dark green against a lightening gray sky. Sun breaks through the cloud cover to brighten a swath of forest on the upper slope of Saddleback Mountain.

Dead trees stand bog-side. Suddenly, something lets fly from a high limb!

A great bird wings over the lake, banks, swoops upward, a shaft of sunlight catching its white head, white tail feathers! A bald eagle! We stand in silence, watching, watching, as it circles above the lake, flashes in and out of the sunlight, makes its way eastward to disappear into the trees on the far eastern shore. Wow.

Time to sit. There is a picnic table here. We drink some water, then sit quietly, looking out. A loon calls. Calls once more. Not bad for a half-rain, half-sun day.

Back we hike to the trailhead and parking area at the yurt. There we meet another couple, visitors from Canada. They, like us, are curious to explore Nordic ski trails in summer. We tell them of wildflowers, the eagle, the sun-lit view over the lake and supreme quiet.

Our outing has covered a bit more than 3 miles, which we have walked in 1 hour and 30 minutes, over largely level ground. Time well-spent!

FIELD NOTES

Rock and Midway Ponds

Rock Pond Trail and Upper Fly Rod Crosby Trail
Sandy River Plantation

Overview: Fairly level to gradually rising, mostly grassy trail, 0.5 mile to Rock Pond (1.0 mile round-trip). Continue 0.3 mile to Midway Pond. Trail narrows in descent to this second pond, the pathway holds step-over rocks and roots. Total round-trip for both ponds: 1.6 miles. Pristine, undeveloped ponds. Wildlife viewing opportunity, particularly in early morning and in late afternoon-evening.

Side trail to two overlooks (Overlook Trail) over ascending, steeper, pathway, provides further option, adds approximately 0.6 miles to a round-trip. Near overlook provides view of Midway Pond and distant Mount Blue. Farther overlook views Rangeley Village and City Cove.

Approach trail to Rock Pond signed as both "Rock Pond Trail" and northern section of "Fly Rod Crosby Trail".

Trailhead: Saddleback Mountain Ski Resort, Rock Pond condominium complex. Drive Dallas Hill Road to Saddleback Mountain Road, reaching the ski lodge. Bear right at the lodge drop-off area, passing large parking lot on the right. Stay left to turn onto Rock Pond. Follow this road uphill in an s-turn. At the top of the turn, stay straight, making no turns through the condominium area. At end of the road boulders block farther passage. A 2–3 vehicle parking area is on the left, with more parking space along the road itself.

To the left of the boulders a number of signs (3 at most recent visit) indicate Rock Pond Trail, and/or Fly Rod Crosby Trail. Walk past the boulders on what is a continuation of the road. In 200′ watch for a Register Box on right. Trail continues straight ahead.

Nearest town: Rangeley

Maps: Delorme *Maine Atlas* Map #29, 1-E; Saddleback Ski Area has published a map that depicts the Rock Pond Trail and other hiking trails on or near the mountain; availability of this map may depend upon its reprinting. Outfitter stores in the town of Rangeley may have copies, or alternate maps; USGS: Saddleback Mountain.

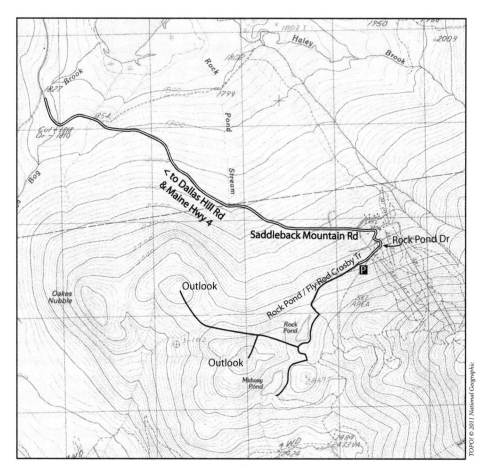

Elevation Gain: less than 100′

On Trail:

All but hidden from distant view, tucked in among foothills off the northern slope of the Saddleback Range, lie two ponds of remarkable beauty—Rock Pond and Midway Pond. A short, 0.9 mile route that takes in both ponds, most of it following the Fly Rod Crosby Trail, follows a moderate grade, making the hike fairly easy.

An added opportunity is a side trail to two overlooks, one above Midway Pond with an exceptional southwest view of the summit cone of Mt. Blue, and the other a look at the eastern end of Rangeley Lake. The overlook trail is short, too, and those who walk both the main and side trails will cover about 1.6 miles to reach Midway Pond.

I have taken this pond hike a number of times when I am in the Rangeley Region—making my way at early morning, mid-day, and at twilight. Each time of day offers a different mood, from the cool brightness of an early summer morning, to the breeziness at noon when I hiked in to sit by Midway for lunch, to an evening stroll to find waters so still that the sunset-touched clouds overhead were mirrored in one pond, then the other.

The trail, a continuation of the road, crosses a ski trail that connects higher terrain with the lower, Magalloway condominium area, and reaches a register box for the Fly Rod Crosby Trail. From this point it is approximately 14 miles south on the Crosby Trail to Reeds Mills in Madrid, and about 8 miles to Maine Highway 4 by way of both the Fly Rod Crosby Trail and the Appalachian Trail. I read in the Register of a winter party that skied to Reeds Mills in a day—and that catches my interest for a future outing.

I continue westward, ascending a wet area where ledge, exposed or lying just under the thin soil, carries water across the trail. Picking my way carefully, I avoid most of the mud. The trail passes an old twitch trail on the left, then enters a predominantly fir forest. A red squirrel chatters in the firs on one of my evening hikes, perhaps curious at a twilight hiker.

In fifteen minutes Rock Pond appears through the trees to the right, and I soon reach the first of three short side trails to Rock Pond. Taking the first, I step to the shore. Indeed true to its name, the pond is ringed with boulders and small rock outcroppings. Water lilies, small bright yellow spheres, dot the surface.

The next side trail is only 10 yards past the first, and is a bit drier. The third trail I reach in another 3–4 minutes. The driest of the three, it affords a view down the full length of the pond.

Beyond this third side trail I arrive at a trail junction for the Overlook Trail, a spur to the right (north). There is a primitive campsite at the junction—simply an old fire ring in the middle of the trail. More about the Overlook Trail in a moment!

For now, I continue on the Fly Rod Crosby Trail, a continuation of the Rock Pond Trail.

I continue westward, leaving Rock Pond behind me, over trail that drier in this section, even as it passes a small bog which lies to the left. Ascending slightly, the trail takes a pronounced right turn, signed, at a junction with an unmarked trail coming in from the left. This left-hand trail is a discontinued cross-country ski trail that looks more traveled than it is because water run-off has scoured the trail bed. Some maps incorrectly show this trail as the Fly Rod Crosby route, but that is not the case. Watch for Fly Rod Crosby Trail diamond shaped trail markers on the main trail.

I continue on the main trail to the next junction—a 3-way intersection. To the left, the Fly Rod Crosby Trail diverges to head southwesterly for 1.0 mile through fairly thick fir growth, on its way to Reeds Mill, many miles distant. To the right (north) at this 3-way junction is another spur to the Overlooks. Straight ahead lies the 0.1 mile path to Midway Pond—my destination.

From the intersection the main trail to Midway descends, with two blow-downs to clamber over, and a third that is skirted by a herd path worn by previous hikers. Soon the pond comes into view—and on a recent twilight hike, what a view! The water lies still and smooth, the fir and cedar shoreline mirrored flawlessly. The last touch of the lowering sun plays orange, rose, and lavender on the clouds overhead—all of this reflected on the water below. It is a strangely beautiful sight. At the far end of the pond the leaves of a solitary red maple have already turned crimson though fall is still weeks away. In the lowering light it stands distinct apart from its dark green conifer neighbors. I stay here for a while—making sure that I had ample light for the remainder of my hike.

A rough trail leads around the perimeter of Midway, but be alert that it is rough. On one of my hikes here I follow this trail to a small point midway on the north shore. I have also made Midway a lunch stop, with a convenient boulder for a seat.

On days when I hike straight from Midway directly back to the trailhead where my truck is parked, I have covered the distance in 30 minutes. That return hike offers more than simply hiking out. As I emerge from the woods and pass the Fly Rod Crosby Trailhead Register box that I passed on my way in, I step out onto a striking viewpoint of the great northwest to northeast sweep of the

Northern Forest. This is the view that lies open to those who stand on the north slope of Saddleback.

Take a look at this—one of the great pristine views in the entire Eastern United States: Saddleback Lake in the foreground, Gull Pond to the northwest, the East Kennebago Range more northerly, and beyond that, Round Mountain, Snow Mountain, and the mountains along the international boundary with Canada. Toward the northeast juts Potato Nubble, then the steep rise to the summits of Saddleback and The Horn, both over 4000′ in elevation. Many a High Peaks Region hike ends in the trees, the views left behind at higher ground. Not so here, where the hike finishes with a flourish—an expansive north country panorama where the deep green of the Northern Forest runs unbroken to the mountain skyline beyond. This is rare and precious mountain country!

Note on the Overlook Spur Trail. The Overlook Trail ascends a low hill to a lookout point over Midway Pond, and continues to the north side of the hill for a view of Rangeley Lake. Each has a rough cedar slab bench at ground level, and nearby rock outcrops, for sitting. Distance is short—about 0.3 miles to the farthest point, the Rangeley overlook—and the side trip is well worth taking. The Midway Pond view is striking—a look over the pond, through a gap in the northwest end of the Saddleback Range, to Mt. Blue. It is an unusual angle of view, framing the upper slopes of southern Franklin County's signature mountain, a former fire tower peak. So clear is the view that I see the observation tower on the summit, constructed in the style of a classic fire tower.

There are two access points from the main trail to the Overlook Trail. One is immediately west of Rock Pond The other is immediately east of Midway Pond at the junction where the Fly Rod Crosby Trail diverges left, skirting the pond about 30 yards above it. I almost always walk to Midway Pond first, taking the main trail. On my return hike, after ascending from Midway Pond back to the 3-way intersection of main trail, Crosby Trail, and Overlook Trail, it is then that I hike the Overlook Spur. If unsure, keep to the main trail and save the Overlooks for another hike.

Perham Stream Birding Trail

East Madrid

Overview: 2.0 mile loop trail (segmented, with shorter and longer distances possible) along Perham Stream, over open ground once pasture and hayfield, and through forest of mixed hardwood-softwood growth. Level to rolling terrain. Fine views north and northwest to the Saddleback Range, and east and northeast toward Mt. Abraham (*Mt. Abram*, locally. Mixture of settings—woodland, open land, and water-bordering—along with southern exposure, offer habitat for more than one hundred species of birds. Bird lists, maps, and trail register at trailhead. Picnic tables along trail.

Spur trails to viewpoints and historic sites, including rural cemetery and site of former schoolhouse and post office.

Trailhead: 553 E. Madrid Road, E. Madrid, Maine. The trailhead is on the East Madrid Road, 4.7 miles from its intersection with Maine Highway 142 north of Phillips. Road turns to gravel before reaching the trailhead. See Delorme *Maine Atlas* Map #19, 3-A. Look for a trail kiosk on the left side of the road immediately after crossing a bridge over Perham Stream. Opposite the trailhead is 553 East Madrid Road. Caretaker lives in farmhouse on the east side of the road, across from Trailhead.

Nearest towns: Phillips (south); Rangeley (north). No food or gasoline services in East Madrid.

Maps: Delorme *Maine Atlas* Map #19, 3-A; Perham Stream Birding Trail Map at Trailhead. USGS: Madrid

Elevation gain: less than 100′

On Trail:

Looking for a fairly gentle hike offering long views toward the High Peaks? How about a rushing mountain stream to provide background music? Throw in a guide to birds commonly found in a habit-rich forest and old pasture? Welcome to the new 2.4-mile Perham Stream Birding Trail in East Madrid, north of Phillips, and South of the Saddleback Range.

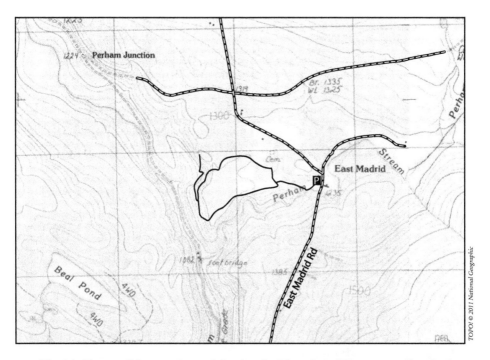

The birding trail is a project of the Sandy River Land Trust, an effort by local Franklin County people to identify exceptional lands in the watershed of the Sandy River, and protect them for recreational and historic value. The Perham Stream Birding Trail, established in 2012, certainly meets those criteria. It offers striking views of the Saddleback Range, to the north, and the Mt. Abraham Range and Farmer Mountain to the east. Nearby Perham Stream rushes down from Mt. Abraham to join Orbeton Stream below the high ground traversed by the trail. This area was once home to a farming community of as many as 60 families, with a post office and school. Today, the combination of fields, replacement forest, and nearby waterways creates ideal habitat for over 100 species of birds.

In recent years I have been exploring the vast peaks and foothills territory immediately south of the Saddleback Range, and north of Madrid. Although the area is well known to local people, and visited on many a family hike, seldom did visitors come here, largely because there were no maintained and publicized trails. In its short history, visitors from as far away as California and Oregon have signed in at the Trail Register for the Perham Stream Birding Trail.

On one visit I take advantage of a guided walk sponsored by the Sandy River Land Trust, led by ornithologist Peter McKinley, with the added presence of Carson Hinkley, owner of the land which the Perham Stream Birding Trail covers. Carson knows the history of the area well, as his is a five-generation East Madrid family, and his running commentary along the way certainly enriched the outing for me. Also on the hike that day are members of the Western Maine Audubon Chapter, and a number of people from all over Maine, from the coast to Range-ley, to enjoy a spring day in the Western Mountains of Maine. I am grateful to

have been in this company, learning of bird life, of the historic farming community of East Madrid, and of the good work of the Sandy River Land Trust.

High peaks loom gray-green to the north and east. Perham Stream glistens in early morning sunlight. Such a day! Let's hike!

We hike west on a gently rising, grassed-over, woods road that crosses the small roadside field. The bird identification begins with a ruby-throated hummingbird buzzing by the trailhead, and robins working the field. Some American crows wing overhead, then out of sight. Mourning doves coo. A pileated woodpecker does a drum roll on a hollow tree, beyond our view.

Nearby Perham Stream swings in close to the edge of the field, affording a view upstream at the rocky waters, then turns south to pursue a steady drop towards Orbeton Stream, out of sight a mile to the west. The trail leaves this first field to enter a new growth forest, regenerating from a wood harvest of about 10 years ago. The hike here is through a "green tunnel"—grassy trail, forest canopy overhead, dappled sunlight falling on the forest floor. Young rock maple and white birch, fir, and pine line the trail.

Emerging from the short stretch of woods, the trail reaches the first of two broad hayfields.

Choices here—short loops provide options for returning to the trailhead for hikes that would total under one mile. I bear left to hike the outer loop of the trail in a clockwise direction, enjoying close-up views of Mt. Abraham and Farmer Mountain from the open field. The route passes through a hollow in the field, then passes into a second, larger field. From here there are fine views of the Saddleback Range, Saddleback Junior on the east end, The Horn in the middle, Saddleback itself to the northwest. The near, low peak to the right (east) of Saddleback Junior is Potato Hill, a near twin to similarly named Potato Nubble which lies north of the Range and therefore out of sight. A broad-winged hawk, on the lookout for field mice, circles overhead, riding the wind currents.

From this field the route continues west, entering the green tunnel once again, reaching a lookout point with views over the Perham Stream Valley, south towards Mt. Blue and southwest to the Tumbledown Jackson Range. Quite a view for a short walk over hayfields and woods paths! Along the walk, and particularly near this stop, we enjoy the song of warblers. Our birding experts identify the songs of black-and-white warbler, magnolia warbler, Nashville warbler, and yellow-rumped warbler in the course of our outing. If some of these have echoes of southern locations, that is because the habitat in this unique setting draws summer visiting birds from the southern USA—and beyond, from the Caribbean.

I am at the extreme southwest limit of the property which the trail covers. From the boundary marker the land slopes sharply to the stream. I learn from Carson Hinkley that when farmers raised cattle on the pastureland of East Madrid generations ago, the cattle were driven across these fields and down this precipitous slope to Perham Stream, to reach the railroad line that ran up Orbeton Canyon. Persuade one critter to start down, and the rest follow!

The birding trail makes no such descent. Instead, the trail makes a 90 degree turn to head north, passing through level woodland once again—over the old cattle-drive route—to reach a spur trail to an overlook above Orbeton Canyon. This 0.2 mile spur should not be missed, as this viewpoint offers the closest Saddleback view of the entire trail system. The south-reaching buttresses of the range stand out in rugged detail. In the planning stage is a new trail, the Berry Pickers Trail, which will ascend one of these buttresses to meet the Appalachian Trail at the Saddleback Ridgeline. (I am told it is expected be open by 2017). Hardy Stream and Orbeton Stream drain the range in this direction, cutting their V-courses into the mountainside.

There was a time when the woods below rang with the sounds of the Sandy River and Rangeley Lakes Railroad, and with the work of loggers whose harvest the railroad shipped to the world beyond. Where I walk today farm families once made their homes. The south-facing ground, the level terrain along the Perham Stream intervale, the dependable water source of Perham and neighbor streams—all this combined to offer much promise to families seeking to make a livelihood in the Maine woods.

The northwest viewpoint marks the outer limit to the trail system. I reverse direction on the outlook spur, return to the main trail. Here I turn left, continuing in a clockwise direction, to pass through woodland, then in and out of open fields, on the way back towards the trailhead. There is more to be seen. A short loop ascends a small hill, rimmed with high white pine—a good spot for sitting. Beyond, a side trail leads to an old cemetery. Beyond this junction, on the main trail, the route continues to the East Madrid Road about 200 yards north of the trailhead.

Here in a small clearing by the road. Carson points to the foundation remains of the post office that once served East Madrid. The village schoolhouse once stood beside it, on the downhill side. Imagine stopping here to pick up the mail—or to go to and from school, the high peaks rising above this mountain intervale! Across the road and beyond a field, lie a pond and marsh—more wildlife habitat!

As for birds, I lost personal count, but my sighting also included blue jay, rose-breasted grosbeak, turkey vultures, kinglet, goldfinch—and a brown thrasher that made an appearance in the roadside field as we returned to the trailhead. Kate Weatherby of Western Maine Audubon was one of the hikers in our group, and she tallied over two dozen birds for the morning walk.

Bring a bird book, binoculars, and lunch. Take time here. Imagine what it was like to live here, farming the land. This is a precious place! Thank you to the

Hinkley family, and to the people of Madrid and the surrounding Sandy River Valley, for making this trail possible, drawing visitors to Franklin County from across the USA!

Many a bird enjoys spending the summer here—join them for a day!

Orbeton Stream Conservation Area
Reeds Mill, Madrid

Overview: Out and back hike along Orbeton Stream, tributary to the Sandy River. Distance of 1.3 mile one way (2.6 mile round-trip) to Perham Stream crossing, with longer or shorter outings possible. Former rail bed for Sandy River and Rangeley Lakes Railroad, with broad walking surface and gradual grade. Land gained conservation status in 2015.

Trailhead: Junction of Reeds Mills Road, Fish Hatchery Road, 50 yards east of bridge over Orbeton Stream. This point is 4.6 miles east of Maine Highway 4 in Madrid. In center of Madrid, turn right over one-lane bridge on Reeds Mill Road (paved). Follow to the bridge, passing 0.1 mile before the bridge the Reeds Mill Church, a landmark.

The conservation route is a multi-use trail, for snowmobiles, skiers, and snowshoers in winter; mountain-bikers, ATV users, and hikers in the warmer seasons. A large signboard and snowmobile trail signs stand at the entrance to the trail.

Park so as not to block the trail, or to obstruct Reeds Mill Road. Ordinarily there is ample room to park along the road. The first 0.5 mile of trail is open to motor vehicle access for camp owners only.

Maps: Delorme *Maine Atlas* Map #19, 3-A. (Orbeton Stream Trail appears on the Delorme map as "Railroad Road" in its lower end; and "Perham Junction Road" as it continues north beyond Perham Stream; USGS: Madrid

Elevation Gain: less than 50′

On Trail:

One spring morning I step out onto the Orbeton Conservation Trail, hoping to watch—and hear—the last of spring run-off rumbling down Orbeton Stream Valley, fed by the snowmelt off Saddleback Range to the North, and Mt. Abraham, Farmer Mountain, and Lone Mountain, to the east and northeast. After passing the few camps scattered along the first half-mile, the stream swings in closer to the rail bed—and I have my wish.

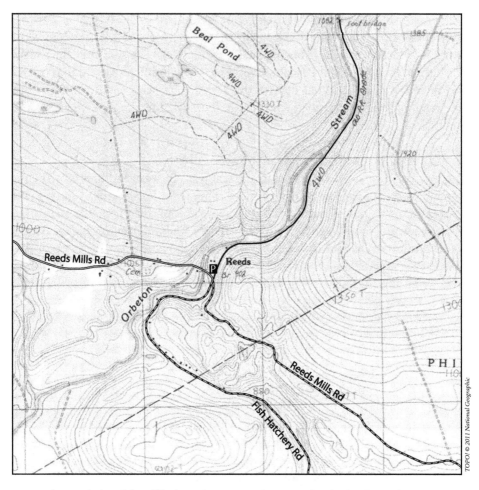

Orbeton is boulder-filled, with many a deep pool. The high peak origins of this stream make for powerful, high flows early in the season, with ample force to dislodge and sweep massive rocks the size of—well, whatever comparison you prefer: Elephants? Large cars? One-car garage? Refrigerators? When the current is sufficiently strong, and it meets more rock and plain earth than it can easily dislodge, it makes a new channel—goes around the obstacle. Over the course of my hike I look out upon an island that has formed from that force. The pulsing river ("Stream" does not adequately describe spring high water) divides in two. I am not hiking at highest water, but I am enjoying the by-product: a wild, noisy course of water, hurrying in the direction of the distant seas.

Trailside forest is mostly fir, with some yellow birch and rock maple, occasional beech, ash, hemlock, and white pine. The walking is straight-forward—literally and figuratively. No roots, no mud, no rocks to clamber over.

Perham Stream announces itself before coming into view. It is a major tributary to Orbeton Stream, draining the broad western slope of Mt. Abraham (Mt. Abram to locals) and neighboring peaks. A curiosity! The sound of the waters rushing over the rocks in Perham Stream has a pitch different from that of Orbeton Stream. Listen. What do you think? It makes sense—different volumes of water, different streambed contours shaped by differences in flow over the centuries.

But a curiosity. Something I easily could miss if I were not keeping silence while hiking. I cross Perham Stream by a footbridge.

Across the way, along the high bluff above the western bank of Orbeton Stream, runs the Fly Rod Crosby Trail, a route from Reeds Mill to Rock Pond and the north slope of Saddleback Mountain. I look for other hikers, but see none. (See my book *Day Hiking in the Western Mountains of Maine* for details on this route.) When hiking on the Crosby Trail in winter by snowshoes, or this Orbeton Route on skis or snowshoes, I have seen bobcat track leading to open water, and moose tracks along the banks. No bobcat or moose today—at least not that I can see.

I suggest Perham Stream as a turn-around point for today's short hike, consistent with the short-outing focus of this book. The railbed continues north for 2.5 miles (additional 5.0 miles round-trip for a total round-trip from Reeds Mill of nearly 8 miles) passing Perham Junction, a sharp turn to the right, eventually reaching a Y-intersection. This is remote country, well beyond the limits of a short hike, and requiring a higher level of gear, water, food, and emergency planning.

The left arm of the "Y" leads to Hardy Stream and the distant west end of the Saddleback Range. The right arm leads to the remote east end of the Saddleback Range. I save such hikes for another day, and possibly a backpack trip rather than a day outing.

Orbeton Stream offers a fine close-up of wild mountain waters! Have a look, and a listen!

Daggett's Rock
Phillips

Overview: 0.5 mile round-trip forest walk to a massive, 3-story high glacial erratic boulder resting on the south slope of Wheeler Hill. Daggett's Rock is also known simply as Daggett Rock, but the former name may be the original, as the rock sits on what was once the farm of a Daggett family. According to information from the Maine Geological Survey (MGS) this great boulder is the largest glacial erratic in Maine, measuring 80′ long, 30′ wide, and 25′ high. Estimated weight is 8000 tons! According to the MGS, tourists—including international visitors—began to visit the site in considerable numbers in the 1800s. Ladders once provided tourist access to the top, but are no longer on site. The MGS website displays cups made in Germany that feature drawings of the rock.

Trail to Daggett's Rock is over a steadily rising old woods road, first through old growth forest, then new growth forest, offering fine opportunity for identification of a wide variety of hardwood and softwood trees. A circle trail around the rock provides perspectives from many angles.

The boulder itself is the principal attraction. Before surrounding hardwood trees leaf out in spring, and after the leaves have dropped in the fall, some views are available south and west toward the Sandy River Valley. This is one of the shortest hikes in this book. I suggest allowing time to explore—and ponder. Do walk around the rock, first on one direction; then the other, pausing from time to time to observe how the appearance of this great boulder changes—in shape, and in hue as the vantage point changes.

Trailhead: Wheeler Hill Road, 2.4 miles from Maine Highway 142, north of Phillips. "Daggett's Rock" signs posted by Maine High Peaks Coalition at the Wheeler Hill Road intersection. On Highway 142, at 1.7 miles, pass the Parlin Road on the right. Next right is Wheeler Hill Road, which begins as paved, and becomes gravel. On the drive in, look to the right for almost "reach-out-and-touch" view of Mt. Blue, distinguished by the summit tower. Parking area on crest of a hill, on right side of the road. The "No Trespassing" sign by the parking area refers to the adjacent property, not the parking spot.

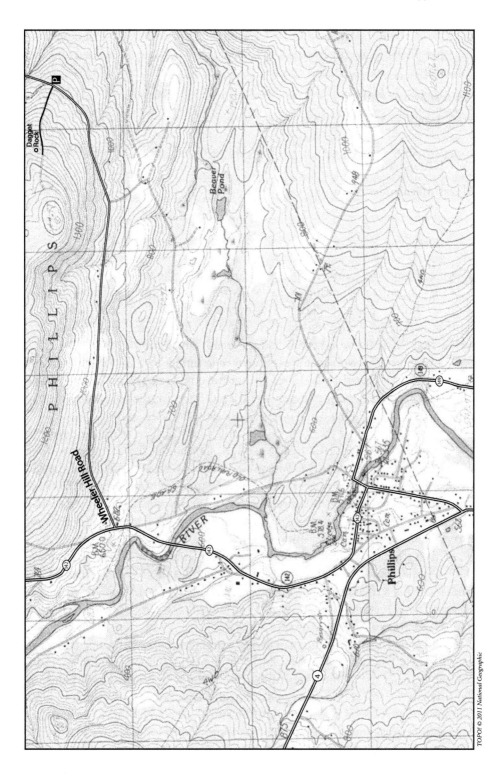

TOPO! © 2011 National Geographic

The trail to Daggett's Rock is across the road. Watch for a sign on an old, high-rising, sugar maple, at the corner of Wheeler Hill Road and the trail.

Nearest Town: Phillips

Map: Delorme *Maine Atlas* Map #19, 3, 4-A; USGS: Phillips

Daggett's Rock does not appear on these maps, but Wheeler Hill Road is designated.

Elevation gain: less than 100′

On Trail:

O n a sunny later summer afternoon I make the hike to Daggett's Rock with my Chocolate Labrador Retriever "Moose" for company. Moose is on a leash, as this is a popular hike, and we expect to see other visitors—and this is deer, snowshoe hare, and red squirrel country. A breeze rustles the high hard-woods that shade the woods road that serves as trail. A good day!

As we enter the woods, a grassy farm road enters to the left. Our route is straight ahead, framed by old growth hardwoods: rock (sugar) maple, white birch, yellow birch, American beech—and a nice surprise, red oak. Some of these extend 70–100′ high. One white birch l estimate to be 2 feet across!

The softwoods have their own statements to make. One white pine reaches 100′. A nearby hemlock rises nearly as high, standing at the corner of a stone wall opening that once provided wagon access between a hayfield and the old road along which the dog and I make our way. Stone walls in the woods indicate that the land had once been cleared for hay or grain crops. When the hey-day of mountain farming in Maine passed, following the Civil War, forests have re-turned to this once-cleared ground.

This is a great trail for tree identification! Do come here at foliage season—the many hardwoods in all manner of color, alongside the deep green of the conifers. Bring a tree book, such as *Forest Trees of Maine,* published by the Maine Forest Service. It contains full view color photos of each tree, along with close up photos of bark, and of leaves or needles.

Midway along the trail the road makes a slight jog to the left, entering a new-growth forest where most trees are but 3–4 inches in diameter. There are more red oak here, joined by the opportunistic hardwoods that spring up when sun-light strikes the forest floor—striped (moose) maple, alders, gray birch in large numbers. A surprise is a Norway pine, an introduced tree. I have learned that immigrants from Europe brought Norway Pine and Norway Spruce to this part of Maine. There are stands in Madrid and in Rangeley, which makes it plausible that I am looking at the descendant tree from one of those immigrant plantings generations ago.

The trail is short, only a quarter-mile. I round the last bend—and there it is!

A great, gray, rounded, mass of solid rock, 3 stories high, 40' across, resting in a clearing, in the middle of the woods. It looks entirely out of place, as though dropped on the way to somewhere else—which is essentially what happened!

About 11,000 years ago, a glacier, up to one mile thick, which had been dragging the massive rock, retreated up this ancient hillside, and let go of it. One moment just the right combination of circumstances prevailed—steep slope, multi-ton boulder, an ever-so-slightly weakening grip of ice to stone. There are thousands of these so-called glacial erratics (the root word for erratic means to wander) across Maine and New England, and north into Canada. Many are the size of a bale of hay, others as large as a corncrib. Daggett's Rock is one of the largest in Eastern North America.

A worn trail circles the rock. Moose the dog and I walk clockwise. Then we retrace our steps, counter-clockwise, angling for different views of this intriguing glacial-age specimen. The rock is split along a north-south line, an ancient fracture so wide that we are able to walk through it. Another split runs east-west through one of the halves. This is narrower, quite a squeeze, and I decide against the attempt as I do not want to face extracting a dog from its narrow confines.

Stand back and have a look at these ancient splits in the rock. I watch the afternoon sun and shade throw patterns on the great gray mass of stone. These splits, shaped by ice, water, and wind, remind me of slot canyons in the high desert country of the American Southwest.

The forces that broke the rock are, of course, still at work. There are other cracks, some small, some large enough that out of them grow small birch and maple. Their roots will advance the expanding of the cracks in which these trees have emerged, letting in more water, leading to more ice—and the story goes on.

We circle the Rock one more time. It is now that I notice the growth around its perimeter. Sumac hold scarlet plumes that bob ever so lightly in the afternoon breeze. More red oak, aspen ("popple" to Mainers), beech, moose maple with oversized duck-foot leaves, and small balsam fir. In our circling I see the Rock in a different way from each vantage point—different light draws my attention to angles, indentations, more cracks. On close inspection the rounded rock is intricately patterned, and far from smooth. An old truth—walk slowly in the woods, or simply sit still for a time—and things hidden from sight at first viewing, will be revealed.

Uh-oh! In a small clearing to the left of the rock—and off the path around the rock—grows poison ivy. Watch for distinctive three pale-green leaves, with a red dot at the center where the leaves join. I missed seeing that on the first few times around! There is ample room to avoid it, and I do.

We amble back down the shaded trail to the trailhead. I don't know what is on the mind of my canine companion, but my thoughts run to the first human to come upon this great mass of rock so deep in the forest, and to the forces of nature over time—and to what a joy it is to spend an hour or so of a sunny summer afternoon, walking along an old woods road in the foothills of the Western Mountains of Maine.

FIELD NOTES

Bigelow-Flagstaff Region

The 17 mile long Bigelow range, and Flagstaff Lake, Maine's fourth largest, are the major features. Fed by run-off from the Bigelow Range, other mountains that rim Flagstaff Lake, and north lying tributaries draining from near the international border with Quebec, Dead River plunges over Grand Falls, reached by a 0.9 mile hike from remote-lying logging roads. Cathedral Pines, located on an old floodplain northwest of the lake, and the southeast shores of the lake, offer a series of forest, lakeside, streamside walks in a region of particular historic interest—ranging from Benedict Arnold's march to Quebec in 1775, and the flooding of the towns of the Dead River Valley in 1950 when the Dead River was dammed to store water for electricity generation.

Hikes here include trails of Maine Huts and Trails System, the Appalachian Trail, and the Bigelow Preserve.

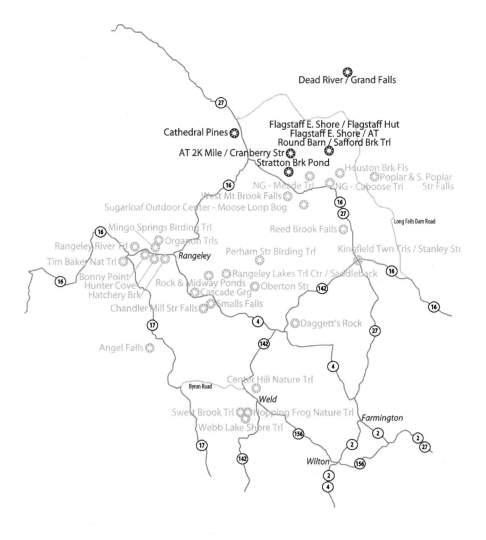

Dead River / Grand Falls

27

Cathedral Pines

Flagstaff E. Shore / Flagstaff Hut
Flagstaff E. Shore / AT
Round Barn / Safford Brk Trl

AT 2K Mile / Cranberry Str
Stratton Brk Pond

Houston Brk Fls
Poplar & S. Poplar
Str Falls

NG - Meade Trl   NG - Caboose Trl

West Mt Brook Falls

16

Sugarloaf Outdoor Center - Moose Loop Bog

16

27

Long Falls Dam Road

Mingo Springs Birding Trl

16

Organon Trls

Reed Brook Falls

Rangeley River Trl

Rangeley

Perham Str Birding Trl

Kingfield Twn Trls / Stanley Str

Tim Baker Nat Trl

16

16

Bonny Point /
Hunter Cove
Hatchery Brk

Rock & Midway Ponds

Rangeley Lakes Trl Ctr / Saddleback

Cascade Grg

Oberton Str

142

16

Chandler Mill Str Falls

Smalls Falls

17

4

Daggett's Rock

27

Angel Falls

142

4

Center Hill Nature Trl

Byron Road

Weld

Sweet Brook Trl   Hopping Frog Nature Trl

Farmington

Webb Lake Shore Trl

156

2

2

17

142

Wilton

156

2

2

2

27

2

4

Grand Falls

Township 3, Range 4
Bingham Kennebec Purchase West of Kennebec River

Overview: 0.9 mile one-way walk (1.8 mile round-trip) to dramatic, Niagara-shaped falls 40′high and over 100′across. Grand Falls sits at the head of the Lower Dead River gorge, a half-mile below the site of the former Dead River Dam. A rock perch offers a fine viewpoint facing the falls nearly head-on from 100′away.

Remote location, reached by 17.4 mile drive over logging roads to the trailhead.

Note: Grand Falls may also be reached on foot over the Maine Huts and Trails (MHT) system, but the hiking distances are long—over 14 miles round-trip from Big Eddy area on Long Falls Dam Road—and therefore not described here. See *Day Hiking in the Western Mountains of Maine, Second Edition* 2015; or *Snowshoe and Cross-Country Ski Outings in the Western Mountains of Maine*, 2016, for descriptions of 3-season, and winter season access, respectively, via the MHT system.

Trailhead: Grand Falls Road gate, 7.4 miles from Big Eddy Road/North Flagstaff Road. The turn-off to Grand Falls Road is 10.0 miles east of Maine Highway 27 in Jim Pond Township. Total driving distance from Highway 27 (Big Eddy Road plus Grand Falls Road) one-way is 17.4 miles. Allow a minimum of 45 minutes each way, and expect to drive 25 miles per hour, or less.

From Stratton Village, drive north on Highway 27 past Eustis and Cathedral Pines. After crossing the town line into Jim Pond Township, look for the Big Eddy Road—a right turn. The opening to this graveled road is quite broad—one of its distinguishing features as travelers look for the turn-off.

The Grand Falls Road is a left turn 10.0 miles from Highway 27. A hand-lettered sign and snowmobile route signs for ITS 89/86 indicate the turnoff. The snowmobile trails and Grand Falls Road coincide as far as the Shaw Pond Road, where ITS 89/86 diverge from Grand Falls Road. At some intersections signs direct the way to Grand Falls. Do carry a map, as there are numerous side roads, some signed, others not.

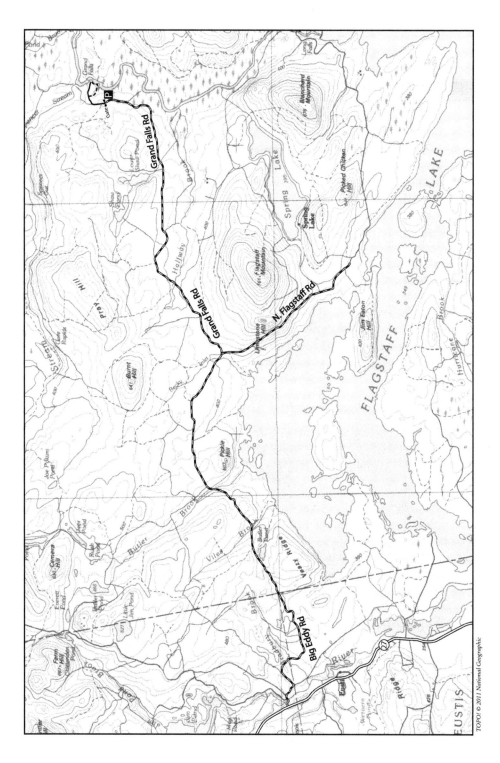

TOPO! © 2011 National Geographic

Caution: Gravel roads off Highway 27 are regularly traveled by log trucks. Be alert. Prepare to yield to trucks approaching or traveling behind. The gravel surface makes braking and turning less responsive than is the case on pavement. Reduce speed. Be vigilant when approaching corners and hills, as the line of sight may be limited. Expect other vehicles any hour of the day or night.

The "trailhead" is at the orange metal gate across the Grand Falls Road 7.4 miles from the Big Eddy Road. Gate is at the crest of a hill. At the base of this hill there is ample parking on either side of the road. Do not park at the gate. *Never block any gate or road anywhere in the Maine woods, no matter how remote the area.* Logging equipment and emergency vehicles may require access anywhere, at any time.

Nearest Towns: Eustis, including Village of Stratton. Gas up before driving this route. Carry food and water. No services on this remote road.

Maps: Delorme *Maine Atlas* Map #29, 2-B, 3-A, 5-A; Maine Huts and Trails Map—for trail configurations near the falls; USGS: Basin Mountain

Elevation Gain: Negligible

On Trail:

It is a bright fall day when my wife and I make our first visit to Grand Falls by way of the Grand Falls Road route. I have been to the falls a number of times in winter, skiing in on the Maine Huts and Trails routes from Long Falls Dam Road, or from West Forks, and have hiked in summer from Long Falls Dam Road—but had not yet approached by this shorter route.

With a close eye on our maps, we reach the metal gate on the Grand Falls Road—which at this point coincides with snowmobile trail ITS 86—that marks the end of the drive and beginning of our walk. We hike the low hill from where we have left our truck to the crest where the gate is located, past the gate, and down the other side. Immediately on our left at 0.1 mile the graveled Philbrook Road intersects with our route—bringing in ITS 89/86 again.

Our direction is straight ahead along the fir-bordered road to a junction at 0.4 miles where the ITS 89/86 snowmobile trail continues straight ahead. *Pine Loop, the way to Grand Falls, is a 90 degree turn to the right.*

Fir predominates, but maple, birch, and the copper-leafed beech are among the mix, with an occasional high pine. Chickadees, juncos, and blue jays busy themselves in the woods. Afternoon sun warms our walk. A fine day for a walk in the Maine woods—with the best yet to come.

At 0.5 miles from the trailhead gate an unsigned woods road enters from the left, and at 0.6 miles there is a turn-off to the right that leads to a private camp. We continue straight, as Pine Loop descends towards the falls—which are well out of sight, but now within earshot. Apart from our footfalls on dry leaves of maple and birch, above our conversation, there runs a steady, low roar—Grand Falls.

A snowmobile stop sign—deep in the Maine woods—marks the next junction. Although we are no longer on ITS 89/86, Pine Loop serves as a spur snowmobile trail for riders visiting Grand Falls in winter. We are 0.8 miles into our walk. Here the Maine Huts and Trails route west toward Flagstaff Hut and east toward Grand Falls Hut crosses our road (signs). To the right (south) on the MHT trail lies the Dead River bridge, the Tom and Kate Chapell footbridge, used by hikers, skiers, and those on snowshoes. The bridge is a point of interest, 0.1 mile away, and offering a view of the remnants of the former Dead River Dam, now essentially a series of rock piles in the river. To the left, that trail continues west, then north, to circumvent the falls, on the way to the Grand Falls Hut of MHT, 1.2 miles distant.

Within 50 feet our road divides at a "Y" intersection, with the two arms eventually forming a loop at the edge of the falls (As in "Pine Loop"). Either way, the falls are no more than 0.1 mile farther. We choose the right, descend—with the sound of the falls now loud and imposing—step out from our green tunnel of tree canopy, and here we are! Wow!

The dark purple-black of the river, in one broad, smooth flow above the falls, drops out of sight. Spray flies! We shout to be heard!

For a closer view we hike on to the very end of the loop, where a blue-blazed footpath leads east up a short slope, reaching a rock pulpit-like perch affording a near straight-on look at the wild maelstrom of Grand Falls. At center a great mass of water plunges into a broad pool below. To the right, more current races through a chute, spills onto a great, black rock mass below, with its own roaring pitch. Such contrast! A quiet road walk deep in the woods; then, suddenly, massive falls, turbulent, roaring, spray-flinging! Quite the sight!

Our vantage point above the falls is a good 100 feet from the center of the turmoil, but the air around us fills with spray. In winter, the spray freezes, coating trees well away from the river with lacey coatings of ice. Great pine, cedar, fir, spruce, and hemlock thrive along the river banks, well-watered. Now the droplets rain lightly down upon us, even as we stand in the light of the afternoon sun.

Surprise! Amidst the tumult, a rainbow! Half-way up the falls, afternoon sun plays on the spray-filled air. What a gift—all the colors of a rainbow, hovering just over the falls! This on a bright, and cloudless day!

These falls, with their breadth and height, and the great volume of water carried in the Dead River, are the most massive in Western Maine, and one of

the largest—might I say "grandest"—in the state. They are well worth seeing—whether by our itinerary today—a long road in, followed by a short hike; or by hiking or skiing the entire way from an MHT distant trailhead.

Hikers who wish to explore the area upstream of the falls may walk a short 0.1 mile out and 0.1 mile return route on the Maine Huts Trail heading west to the Chappell Bridge, about 0.2 mile upstream. Walk back up Pine Loop to this trail junction, marked by prominent trail signs. West is the direction towards Long Falls Dam Road and Flagstaff Hut.

Walk west towards the footbridge, a sturdy iron structure that offers good views upstream and down. As mentioned above, look for a series of rock islands upstream. These are of human design, part of the former Dead River Dam. This dam held back logs that had been harvested, and were kept here to be released downstream at optimum water levels. Eventually these logs would be processed at mills in Madison, Skowhegan, Waterville, and other points south along the Kennebec River. The last log drive on the Kennebec was in 1974. Trucking replaced log drives, as a long chapter in the history of the Maine woods drew to an end, with its stories of log-drivers with pick-poles, wearing hope-nail boots doing the harrowing work of freeing up log jams. Men walked out onto the logs they were about to dislodge, anticipating the moment when their pick-pole work would break-up the jam, and there was just enough time to run across the now-moving logs for shore before the mass would accelerate to river-speed.

Recall that chute on the right side of Grand Falls? Logs would become hung up on the craggy rock formation on this side, creating jams that few loggers wanted to approach. The solution was to blast this chute, widening an existing gap into one broad enough to minimize the chances of log jam.

Downstream from the Chappell Bridge the river makes a left turn. A wooded promontory at the turn blocks the view of Grand Falls, and the waters here appear curiously calm—but there is no mistaking the great roar emanating from the cataract beyond. Attend closely to the farthest point downstream, as this is a deer crossing area. I have seen deer swim the river both summer and winter. It is quite the sight.

Return by the same 0.1 route to the Pine Loop Road, to then hike back 0.9 mile to the parking area on the Grand Falls Road.

Yet another option when returning from the short 0.1 walk to the bridge, is a blue-blazed trail that leads 0.15 mile through the woods, just in from the shore, coming out above the falls at Pine Loop. This trail affords a river-level view. The surrounding terrain forms a bowl, echoing the crashing and thundering of the dashing water as it slides smoothly over the lip of falls, then—boom—plunges out of sight. As I stand immediately upstream, I see nothing of the foot of the falls themselves—but proof positive of their existence a mere few feet away is the leaping, far-flung spray that fills the air with a fine mist.

Needless to say, I do not advise entering the water above the falls to wade or to swim! The pulsing river has scoured a steep drop-off, and the current is swift and powerful.

Where the blue blazes meet the Pine Loop Road, turn left. In a few steps you will pass the intersection with the Maine Huts Trail. Continue on Pine Loop Road to Grand Falls Road, and back 0.9 mile to the parking area.

Quite the spot! Behold the power of water!

Cathedral Pines Pathways

Eustis

Overview: Options of 1.0 up to 2.0 miles (or more) of forest walk on level pathways, beneath the high canopy of a 300 acre stand of 80′ high red pine—a setting of remarkable beauty. Three main trails: Blue, Red, and Yellow, offer out-and-back or loop hikes. An extension of the Blue Trail is "The Boardwalk", which leads west beyond the pines into a mixed hardwood-softwood forest featuring white birch, beech, and red maple, along with cedar and fir—and to a broad bog traversed by 0.2 mile of plank bridging (hence the name "The Boardwalk"). Bigelow Range view from the bog.

To imagine the trail network, think of a circle with a 2-mile circumference (The Yellow and Red Trails, each a half-circle, joined at either end) bisected by a 0.5 mile straight path (The Blue Trail). Beyond the Blue Trail, and beyond the circle, extends the Boardwalk, which leads out of the pines to reach the bog referred to above.

The expansive level ground, evidence of an ancient flood plain, is unusual in this region of rugged peaks and rolling foothills. Come here on a hot day to hike in the cool shelter of the pines. Choose these trails on a chilly and blustery day when the pine stand acts as wind break. Watch sunlight filter through the pines, at sunrise, mid-day, sunset—anytime of day.

Trailhead: Intersection of Eustis Ridge Road with Maine Highway 27; 3.6 miles north of Highway 16/27 intersection in Stratton Village; 2.9 miles north of the Boat Launch on Highway 27; directly across Highway 27 from Cathedral Pines Campground (Address 945 Arnold Trail Highway); and 0.1 mile south of Pines Market. Wooden sign for Cathedral Pines Trails. Metal gate. Parking area to right of gate.

Please do not block this gate, or any other gate in the Maine woods, no matter how remote the location. Emergency vehicles may require access at any hour of the day or night, any day of the year.

Picnic and toilet facilities available in season across the highway at Cathedral Pines Campground, or at Pines Market. Eustis Public Beach accessed through campground.

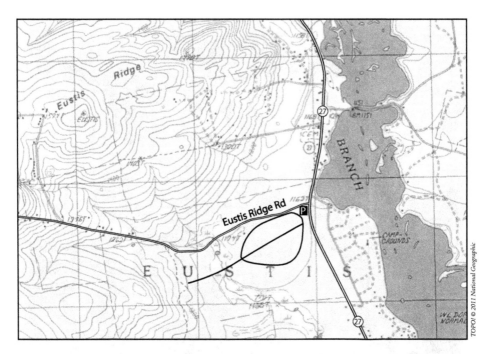

Nearest Town: Stratton Village (south); groceries and gas available 0.1 mile north on Route 27, Eustis.

Maps: Delorme *Maine Atlas* Map #29, 2-B; trail maps posted at trail intersections; Pines Pathways map, available from Cathedral Campground and on-line; USGS: Stratton

Elevation Gain: Negligible. All trails are on level ground.

On Trail:

Cathedral Pines is a setting unlike any other in Western Maine, a wonder among scenic wonders—great red pines; needle-strewn shaded forest floor; the light—indirect, muted. To what might I compare it? Of course, the very name, "cathedral" is apt for the high ceiling/canopy, the light parsing through that canopy as through high windows, and a pervasive quiet. I recall walking the Muir Woods in California, which has much taller and older trees, yet has a similar touch of gentle light amidst the mightiness of soaring pines. Some visitors might recall the great pine forest stands in the Deep South—Mississippi and Alabama, for example.

After many a trip to Flagstaff Lake, to the Bigelow Range, to the North Branch of the Dead River, Chain of Ponds, Snow Mountain—all of these mag-

nificent wild places so near to Cathedral Pines, I finally make the first of what would be many stops here to walk these gentle pathways. The trails, level as they are, make for a relaxed and relaxing hike, and take little time. But I give the Pines their due on this first day, taking my (sweet) time. In the course of that first day, a fall afternoon, I walk every step of every trail in the Pines, pausing now and then to take a seat on one of many benches built between close-standing trees.

On the cool, clear afternoon I have chosen, I have the trails to myself. I park in the parking area to the right of the gate, by the corner of Eustis Ridge Road, and head out on the Blue Trail, marked by rectangular signs simply painted a dark blue. The high red pines are the dominant species of tree in the stand. Their high canopy shades the dark red-brown needle-covered forest floor, which lies free of undergrowth. The trail itself, wide and level, arrows in a straight line westward through the forest. First impressions? Quiet. That—and the muted light. Quite a spot.

In 50 yards I reach an intersection where the Red Trail diverges to the right (north) to begin a great 0.8 mile arc that ends at a farther intersection with the Blue Trail. To the left (south) the Yellow Trail makes its own arc, with a turn or two, over 1.2 miles to meet the Blue and Red Trails. Walking the two trails as a loop would be a 2.0 mile walk.

My choice is to continue straight ahead on the Blue Trail. The soft forest floor absorbs my footfalls. I pad through the forest as though moccasin-shod, making barely a sound. I pass the first of many benches built between close-standing pines, stop, sit, watch, listen. Resuming my walk, in 10–15 minutes I cover the 0.5 miles to reach a clearing and the western junction of the Yellow and Red Trails. The Yellow Trail enters from the left. The Red Trail enters from the right.

A large sign welcomes visitors to the Cathedral Pines—its location here suggesting "You have arrived at the heart of this great forest! Enjoy!"

I do plan to hike the loop of the Red and Yellow routes this day, but first continue straight ahead, westward, past the clearing, on the Boardwalk spur that leads to a broad bog. This trail exits the red pine stand, passes a metal gate, and enters a mixed growth forest of cedar, fir, white birch, and maple. The footpath changes from pine litter to dirt and gravel—and in 100′ to planking that stretches far into the distance over wet ground bordering the bog, and to the bog itself. Much hard work went into this boardwalk!

The bog—what a contrast to the pine stand! Tawny grass, bright in the sun, billows in a breeze that I never felt back amidst those pines. As the planked trail approaches the bogstream, beyond the initial wet border sections, I gain a look at the Bigelow Range to the southeast.

On I go, over the full length of the spur trail, cross the bog stream, and wind around the only curve I have encountered on this route. In 0.1 mile beyond the stream, I reach the end of the footpath at a gate bordering a snowmobile trail. Time to reverse direction. Back over the planking and the bog once more—one more good look at the Bigelow Range before I re-enter the forest.

Now that I know of this view, I will look for Cathedral Pines and this west-lying bog the next time I hike North Horn in the Bigelow Range. A favorite of mine for its northward view, the peak of North Horn is reached by a 0.2 mile spur trail off the Appalachian Trail. Like the bow of a ship, this pyramid summit juts in the direction of the North Branch of the Dead River, points over and beyond Flagstaff Lake, and offers a look at distant Chain of Ponds and the peaks that lie along the international border with Quebec.

Back at the clearing I left when taking the bog spur trail, I turn right (south) on the Yellow Trail to hike its full length. I am back under the red pines once again, moving quietly over a foot path of pine needle duff—as soft a trail bed as I have ever known. To my right, towards the southwest, the lowering afternoon sun throws long shadows over the forest floor. Cathedral, indeed.

The Yellow Trail follows a twitch road south and east for 0.9 miles before leaving that road at a sharp left turn, to return to meet the Blue Trail near the trailhead and parking area.

Time now for the Red Trail! I walk this route, which roughly parallels Eustis Ridge Road, for 0.5 mile under the pines before turning west at a four-way intersection with a former ATV-snowmobile trail. Be alert here, as the Red Trail makes a sharp left turn, and the red trail marker to the left stands at the edge of my peripheral vision. I scan the intersection for a red marker, look far down each of the four trails—and there it is, the now familiar bright red. (First time visitors walking the loop may find this intersection a bit clearer to navigate by walking the Yellow Trail to the Red Trail, i.e. walk in a clockwise direction from the trailhead by the parking area.)

More walking in the shadows of the pines and I reach the west junction of the Red Trail with the Yellow Trail and the Blue Trail. I turn left (east) on the Blue Trail, to return to the trailhead.

My afternoon walk has taken me the full length of the Blue and Boardwalk trails, and around the great loop formed by the Yellow and Red Trails.

A place apart!

East Shore Flagstaff Lake and Flagstaff Hut

Maine Huts and Trails
Carrying Place Township and Dead River Township

Overview: Eastern end of Flagstaff Lake. 2.0 mile one-way (4.0 miles round-trip) walk over level to gradually rising ground on one of two nearly parallel trails: (1) a wide cross-country ski trail, 100′ in from the lake over much of its length; or (2) a shoreline hiking trail with views westward across Flagstaff Lake, and to the Bigelow Range.

This hike exceeds the usual 2.0 mile round-trip distance limit for walks in this book. I include it because of its relatively gentle nature, and for the exceptional views across Flagstaff Lake.

The ski trail route (See (1) above.) is mostly level, and walkers who travel one mile in 30 minutes may expect to reach the Flagstaff Hut in one hour. If your typical time per mile varies from that 30 minute standard, plan accordingly.

A fine hike is available along the shore of the lake (See (2) above), on the Shore Trail, a traditional hiking path that parallels the ski trail, but is out of sight of it. Distance is virtually the same: 2.0 from trailhead to hut.

If planning to walk all the way to the hut, allow time for views at the point just north of the hut, and to visit the hut itself—remembering that a 2.0 mile walk remains to return to the trailhead. If walking in the afternoon, allow time to return to the trailhead before dark, and carry a map and headlamp.

For more detail concerning the area around the Hut and alternate trails, see *Day Hiking in the Western Mountains of Maine, Second Edition* 2016.

Both trails lead to Flagstaff Hut of the Maine Huts and Trails System, year-round lodges that offer accommodations and meals, hot showers, and a gathering room, with services and rates varying according to season. Day hikers welcome to come inside to see the facility, and to purchase lunch, baked goods, and hot or cold beverages, in season. Look-out

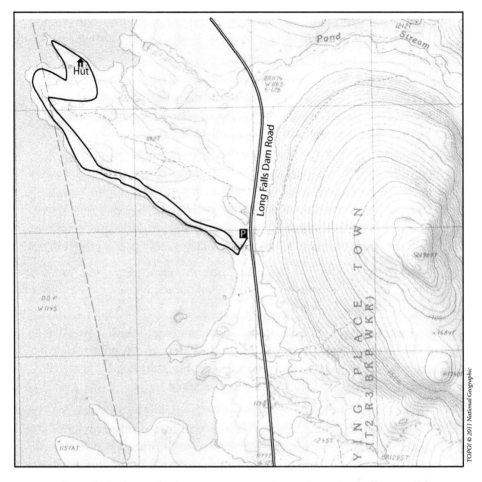

point 0.1 mile from hut offers long views west and north across the lake. Kayaks and canoes available in season by purchasing a Day Membership.

No dogs allowed in the hut, and no dogs permitted on MHT trails December through April.

Bring a pair of inside footwear, or be prepared to walk inside in socks, as footwear worn outside is not permitted inside the hut for cleanliness purposes.

Of all the MHT huts open at this writing—Stratton Brook, Poplar, Grand Falls, and Flagstaff, this hut—Flagstaff—has the shortest approach from an MHT trailhead and the most level terrain. Accordingly, I include it here.

For a description of hiking and ski routes to all four huts, please see *Day Hiking in the Western Mountains of Maine, Second Edition,* 2015; and *Snowshoe and Cross-Country Ski Outings in the Western Mountains of Maine,* 2016.

For paddling routes to Flagstaff Hut and paddling opportunities associated with Stratton Brook Hut, see *Kayak and Canoe Outings in the Western Mountains of Maine,* 2015.

Trailhead: Remote location in Carrying Place Township, near east shore of Flagstaff Lake. The trail departs from the Long Falls Dam Road, 22.8 miles north of the intersection of Maine Highway 16 and the Long Falls Dam Road in the village of North New Portland. The Long Falls Dam Road (paved) passes through Lexington Township, Highland Plantation, and an eastern corner of Carrabassett Valley, before passing the trailhead.

No services on this road. There is a seasonal campground in Lexington. North New Portland has a general store and diner. Nearest gas stations are in Kingfield and Embden.

A waypoint is the East Flagstaff Road, angling to the left (west), 0.3 miles before entering Carrying Place Township, and approximately 4.5 miles before the MHT trailhead. The East Flagstaff Road is graveled, with a small sign indicating "Bigelow Preserve."

The MHT trailhead and parking area is marked by a sign on the Long Falls Dam Road. Here find a kiosk with trail map display, copies of MHT System maps, and a vault toilet. The trails to the hut start at the southwest corner of the parking area, by the kiosk. In 0.2 miles reach a 4-way trail intersection. Turn right for the ski trail route to Flagstaff Hut. Go straight ahead to reach the shore of Flagstaff Lake, and the Shore Trail to Flagstaff Hut.

The distance to the hut from this point is 1.8 miles by either route, for a total one-way hike from the trailhead of 2.0 miles (4.0 miles round-trip).

Nearest Town: North New Portland (grocery store and diner; no gas)

Maps: Delorme *Maine Atlas* Maps #29, 5-B, C; and #30, 1-B, C; Maine Huts and Trails System Map; The Valley Below, available from High Peaks Information Center, Highway 16, Carrabassett Valley; USGS: Little Bigelow Mountain

Elevation Gain: less than 100'

On Trail:

I hike this route often, whether on a short family walk into the Flagstaff Hut, or as part of a longer outing on the MHT system. The views across Flagstaff Lake, and up to the Bigelow Range are extraordinary.

On my most recent outing, my wife and I choose this for our fall foliage trip—and such a day it is! The maples, and the attendant white and yellow birch, popple, and beech—and moose maple, sumac, and blueberry bushes, are at the peak of their fall colors. The October day is bright, clear, and cool enough for us to walk with flannel shirts, though we carry down sweaters and wind shells in our day packs (and sandals for walking inside the hut).

Typical for us is to walk the Shore Trail to the hut, and the main trail/ski trail back to the parking area. When we reach the 4-way intersection 0.2 miles from the trailhead, we continue straight towards the lake, to the intersection with the Shore Trail. Before we head onto that trail, we step to the shore. Here *dry-ki*— fresh water driftwood—has collected, driven by the prevailing northwest winds that drive white-cap waves down the lake in our direction on many a day. On this day the waters stir in a light breeze, and the big waves, at least for the moment, are at rest.

The two highest peaks of the Bigelow Range loom large to the southwest: Avery Peak, 4088', and West Peak, 4150'. Beyond them trail the west-lying peaks of the Horns, and Cranberry peak. To their left (east) rises Little Bigelow, not very little at 3070', with a 2-mile ridge, but smaller in comparison with its more elevated neighbors. Quite the sight.

We poke about the driftwood and the smoothed sand of the lakeside beach—known as "Mile Beach", a rocky shoreline at high water, but offering small stretches of sand in late summer and in fall when lake levels drop.

Returning to the trail we walk north, where frequent gaps in the trees offer more lake views—which change as our vantage point changes—sometimes we are in a white birch-bordered cove; other times at a rocky point. As we move northward, we pass a connector trail that links to the ski trail, to the right; and a short spur left to a lakeside campsite of the Bigelow Preserve.

The Shore Trail brings us through forest of balsam fir and northern cedar, crossing a mix of dry ground and boggy conditions common near the shorelines of northern lakes. We swing more northeastward, enjoying a view left-to-right of Flagstaff Mountain, Picked Chicken Hill (imagine this now forested-shape when cut clear of trees), and Blanchard Mountain, with the Long Falls Dam at the far northeast end of the lake. The trail follows the indentation of a cove, passes the short Beaver Trail spur which leads in-land to a small rise and viewpoint, and continues to a peninsula north of the hut. Immediately past the Beaver Trail a path leads to the hut, which may be seen through the trees. Take this shortcut, or continue first to the peninsula. If continuing to the peninsula—and its extensive views, the route back to the hut is evident—it is a peninsula, and there is only one direction to go!

We enjoy the view, and soon enjoy hot soup and warm cornbread at the hut, for purchase.

Other hikers have stopped by, and we swap trail stories—always a good time.

On our way back to the Trailhead, we choose the ski trail. This trail is clearly marked, but do note that 0.2 miles from the hut it makes a 90 degree right turn into the forest. Some hikers miss this turn and end up hiking back to the parking lot by a service road, which is not so scenic as the ski trail. For this reason, first-time visitors may wish to hike in by the ski trail and return by the Shore Trail—reverse of our itinerary. With a trail map in hand, however, the way should be clear either way.

Do carry a map. I advise doing so for all outings.

Flagstaff Lake is a place of remarkable beauty. The trails that parallel its east shore offer a fine hike, all seasons of the year.

FIELD NOTES

Four Round Barn Area Walks — Flagstaff Lake South Shore

Dead River Township

Overview: Four separate walks in the Bigelow Preserve, on or nearby the southeast shore of Flagstaff Lake, with striking views over the lake and up to the Bigelow Range. Walks start from the "Round Barn" parking area, carry-in boat launch, and tent sites, on the East Flagstaff Road. Distances for these walks range from 0.4 mile to 2.0 miles.

Options:

(1) *Safford Brook Trail South*: Out and back 0.5 mile forest and brook-side walk (up to 1.0 mile round-trip), on the Safford Brook Trail *southbound* at the base of the Bigelow Range;

(2) *Safford Brook Trail North—Loop Walk,* 0.7 mile forest and shoreline loop, beginning at Safford Brook Trail *northbound* to shore of Flagstaff Lake, then west along shore to beach at boat launch, returning to starting point by boat launch access road;

(3) *Bigelow Lodge and Lakeshore*: 0.4 mile out-and-back forest walk on access road to Bigelow Lodge site and to nearby lake shore, with lake views;

(4) *Ferry Farm Out and Back:* 2.0 miles roundtrip forest walk to Ferry Farm peninsula on Flagstaff Lake, along woods roads, to quiet cove with views across the lake.

The Round Barn site is named for a barn that stood on the Rand farm in Dead River Plantation. Construction of Long Falls Dam, which went into operation in 1950, resulted in flooding of the low-lying communities of Flagstaff, Dead River, and Bigelow, and surrounding farmland. Homes, barns, school buildings, sawmills, stores, and other buildings were removed, dismantled, or destroyed in preparation. Residents of these three communities moved elsewhere—some to nearby towns such as Eustis.

The massive round structure stood just above the waterline of the newly-formed Flagstaff Lake, but was destroyed in a fire in 1952 during

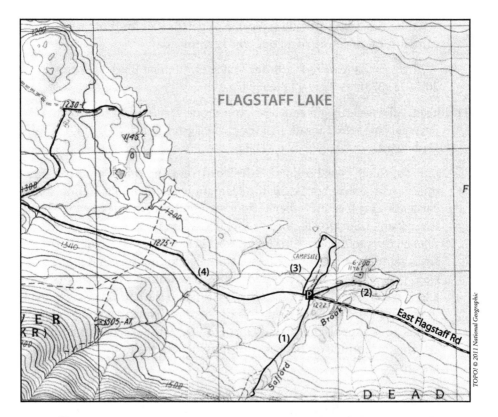

efforts to salvage the barn. At 80′ across and 60′ high, this massive barn with its unusual round shape, was quite the landmark.

In the present day the Round Barn site serves as a trailhead for hiking access to the Bigelow Range via the Safford Brook Trail; as a put-in/take-out point for kayakers and canoeists; and as a tenting and day-use area of the Bigelow Preserve. The combination of views up toward the Range, particularly the nearer summits of Avery Peak and West Peak, and the long views up and down Flagstaff Lake—along with a 100′ sand beach—make this a most attractive spot. Locals refer to the spot as "Round Barn", as in "I am going up to Round Barn this weekend to camp and hike the mountain", even though the barn no longer stands, and the site has grown up in forest.

This is a remote area with primitive walk-in or water-access tent sites and no services. Visitors should come supplied with food and water, with all gear and clothing likely to be needed, with vehicles gassed-up. Designated parking area. Vault toilet near the boat launch.

Walks described provide exploring opportunities for those who are camping, on paddling trips, or come here for a day.

Fire permits required for some tent sites. Contact Bigelow Preserve: 207–778–8231

Trailhead: All 4 walks begin at the Stratton Brook Trailhead, at the Round Barn parking area, 5.0 miles on the East Flagstaff Road, west of Long Falls Dam Road.

From North New Portland, drive north on Long Falls Dam Road 17.5 miles, passing through Lexington Plantation, Highland Plantation, and a corner of Carrabassett Valley. After crossing the town line to enter Dead River Plantation, look for a row of mailboxes on the right and a gravel road angling to the left. This gravel road is East Flagstaff Road. There is a street sign, and a small brown and white sign for Bigelow Preserve. Drive west, passing the Maine Huts and Trails route linking Poplar Hut (south) and Flagstaff Hut (north); the Carriage Road to the left; Bog Brook Road to the right; and an Appalachian Trail crossing. (Note that another entry in this book, Appalachian Trail North to Flagstaff Lake, begins at this crossing.) Continue on the East Flagstaff Road to the Round Barn parking area.

Gas up before approaching this area. Nearest gas at this writing is in Kingfield and Embden. General store/diner in North New Portland. Seasonal private campground, "Happy Horseshoe" in Lexington with small store, limited hours.

Nearest Town: North New Portland

Maps: Delorme *Maine Atlas* Map #29, 5-B (Note: Safford Brook Trail on the Delorme map is an approximation. In reality, the trail crosses the brook, but this crossing is not indicated on this map. Also, the trail continues north of the parking lot 0.2 miles to the lake shore.); Bigelow Preserve Map (Maine Department of Agriculture, Conservation, and Forestry, 207–287–3821, search on line for the above Department and Bigelow Preserve.); *The Valley Below,* map available at High Peaks Information Center, Maine Highway 27, Carrabassett Valley; www.eustismaine.com/ thevalleybelow ; Maine Huts and Trails System Map; USGS: Little Bigelow Mountain.

Elevation Gain: Safford Brook walk, 100'; Flagstaff lake shore walks, negligible gain.

On Trail:

I have visited this section of the Bigelow Preserve on day trips many times, by foot and by paddle (and by snowshoes and cross-country skis) and for many a fine overnight. Our family has come here for day outings to the Round Barn beach, combining swim time, kayak or canoe time on the water, and walking the shoreline.

Safford Brook Walk.

This walk is a gradual ascent through mixed hardwood-softwood forest to approach Safford Brook from the north and west, cross the brook by a footbridge, and continue the ascent to a forested knoll overlook 50' of elevation above the brook. At this point Safford Brook, flowing from drainage below Safford Notch, is joined by a tributary stream. I have taken this walk in mid-August when many seasonal streams are dry, and found Safford Brook to have a good flow of water.

The knoll overlook and the foot bridge are good spots to linger, take a water break, and watch for wildlife. I have continued up the trail beyond the knoll 0.1 mile in a steepening ascent to a spur trail to the left (north) leading to a viewpoint towards Flagstaff Lake. This is a seasonal view, providing the least obstructed look when the maples and other hardwoods have dropped their leaves. In summer there is still a view, but it is limited by the hardwood canopy.

I do enjoy this walk—a good stretch of the legs, particularly if I have been paddling for a time. At high water levels the confluence of streams below the knoll produces a set of small waterfalls and knee-deep pools.

The walk from the Safford Brook trailhead at the Round Barn parking area to the knoll beyond the footbridge is 0.5 miles (round-trip: 1.0 miles).

Above this point the trail steepens considerably, as it climbs to Safford Notch. That hike, and the hike beyond to Avery Peak, are beyond the distances of other walks in this book, and of a greater degree of difficulty—and therefore not described here.

Safford Brook Trail North to Flagstaff Lake/Shoreline Walk to Round Barn Beach.

This section of trail is an historical curiosity. In the years before the construction of Long Falls Dam, when there was no Flagstaff Lake, the Safford Brook Trail served as a route south from Dead River settlement to Safford Notch and to Avery Peak (formerly known as East Peak)—and as a section of the Appalachian Trail. This trail, therefore, once extended northward from the present shore of Flagstaff Lake north to the river and the former location (now below lake level) of the Dead River School. The name of the brook and the trail derives from the Benjamin and Mythel Safford family. The brook and trail crossed their property. Benjamin served as a Maine Forest Service Fire Warden stationed on Avery Peak.

A 0.2 mile section remains, heading northward from the Round Barn parking area to the lake, where it ends at the edge of the water. Walkers may make this an out and back shaded conifer-walk of 0.4 miles. While walking this short distance from parking area to the shore, I cross an old road or lane, a vestige of the days when the area where I walk today was working farmland. An option upon reaching the shore is to turn left (west) to walk along the wooded, irregular shoreline to the Round Barn beach, 0.3 miles, passing through the Round Barn walk-in tent site area.

Out of respect for campers, I walk around—not through—occupied camp sites.

I enjoy this lakeshore walk for the long views across the lake, toward Blanchard Mountain, down the lake beyond the dam; west of Blanchard to Picked Chicken Hill and Jim Eaton Hill; and more directly northward to Flagstaff Mountain. The shoreline walk takes a short jog inland to negotiate a small inlet and draw, before coming out on the beach.

The sandy beach is 100' or more long, a good surprise here in the Maine woods, 100 crow-fly miles from Maine's ocean beaches. Up the lake, where the waters narrow, lies Hurricane Island, once high ground near Hurricane Rips on the Dead River. The island can be difficult to distinguish from the nearby shoreline, but it is there! Binoculars and/or a map of the lake will help.

Back at the beach, notice the sawdust pile past the beach, on shore. Two sawmills operated in this area. Over 65 years since the lake formed and the mills shut down, the pile remains—a reminder of the working life of the people of Dead River, Flagstaff, and Bigelow communities. When the level of the lake water is low, it is possible to see in this area a remnant of the old road that connected Dead River Plantation to Flagstaff Village, to the west and north.

From the beach a broad carry-path leads 100 yards east to a spur road connecting the beach and launch area, and the Round Barn tent sites, to the parking area by the Safford Brook trailhead.

Vault toilets and a signboard with Bigelow Preserve information are located at the end of the loop on this spur road.

Walk 0.2 up the spur road to the trailhead. Total distance for this loop walk: 0.7 miles.

Bigelow Lodge Walk/South Shore of Flagstaff Lake.

Bigelow Lodge is a 3-story building that looks to be lifted from an alpine setting—which provides a clue to its origin. In the 1970s a plan developed to create the largest ski area in the Eastern US on the Bigelow Range. This building was constructed as a prototype lodge. However, an alternate plan arose in the form of a state-wide referendum for the State of Maine to purchase the land to create the Bigelow Preserve. The voters of Maine approved the referendum. The ski area was never built.

Now the lodge functions primarily as crew quarters for work groups in the Preserve. It is *not* open to the public for lodging or day use—except during the winter season, when it is open for day use. Beginning the second weekend in January, and continuing for 10 weekends, the lodge is open for day use on Saturdays and Sundays only, and Monday–Friday during the public school vacation week of Presidents Day in February. Visitors on snowshoes or cross-country skis (or snowmobiles) travel 4.5 miles one-way from where snow plowing of East Flagstaff Road ends near the Appalachian Trail crossing.

For these winter occasions there is usually a fire in the great stone fireplace, and hot water for coffee, hot chocolate, or tea, courtesy of the Maine Bureau of Public Lands. *Prospective winter visitors should contact the Bureau to confirm current schedules and services.*

A *must-see* is the display of photographs from Flagstaff Village and Dead River Plantation taken before Flagstaff Lake flooded the valley. These hang on the inside walls of the lodge, available for viewing by winter visitors. Summer visitors may see another collection of photos and artifacts at the Dead River Historical Society in Stratton Village, open weekends, July and August, 11 a.m.–3 p.m.

The walk to the lodge is a short one from the Round Barn parking area. The northward route is a gravel driveway at the northeast corner of the area. An iron gate 100' down the drive blocks vehicular traffic. I walk around the gate, continue north, and come to a spur road to the right, leading downhill towards the lake. The way to the lodge is straight ahead, not much more than 0.1 mile. Pass a small crew cabin on the right, and arrive at the lodge, which sits in a clearing surrounded by fir, pine, rock maple, and white birch.

Forest has grown up between the lodge and lake, in the years since the lodge was built. Therefore there is little in the way of a view. For that, I return to the driveway to take the spur road to the lake, which is now on my left.

Ordinarily this road gets little use, but is a pathway to the lakeshore for views and a spot or two for a lunch break. See the Safford Brook Trail North entry above for a listing of peaks visible on the northern skyline.

The short walk to the lodge and shore, and return, is about 0.4 miles.

Round Barn West to Ferry Farm Site on Flagstaff Lake.

From the Safford Brook trailhead, walk west towards the spur road leading to the boat launch and tenting area. Do notice the view of Avery Peak to the left, and the sweep of the north slope of the Bigelow Range, running up to the high ground beyond the marsh to the immediate south of the parking area. At the west end of the parking area, continue straight on the woods road. Once a narrow, grassed road, it is now broadened and cleared as a result of a recent timber harvest.

I follow this road for 1.0 mile, with occasional views toward the range, reaching an intersection where a woods road enters from the right, the direction of the lake. Here I turn right, walk for 0.1 mile; then take another right on a worn woods road, to reach the Ferry Farm site, and Flagstaff Lake. If the tent site here is occupied, kindly respect camper privacy. When the site is not occupied, this is a fine spot for a lunch break, a dip or swim, and for views across the lake.

Near the Ferry Farm site vehicles could cross the Dead River by a small ferry, shortening the drive between Dead River farms and homes and Flagstaff Village—or travel back and forth from farmland and wood lots on opposite sides of the Dead River. The river crossing point was flooded when the lake was created from construction of Long Falls Dam.

The small inlet to the right (east) of the site may offer a view of redwing blackbirds amidst willows and alders, black ducks or other waterfowl in the sheltered waters—and the possibility of a nesting loon. As with nesting sites of every kind, when I come upon a loon on the nest, I remain quiet and back away. Watch from a distance, using binoculars. Waterfowl who feel threatened may abandon a nest. Loons may make a ruckus, or, alternately, the adult on the nest may remain completely silent and still, lowering its head to create a low profile. This does *not* mean that the loon does not fear human presence. Quite the opposite. The loon is threatened, and takes the defensive action—of lying low to become inconspicuous as it protects the nest.

Look in the canopy for an osprey nest, and above the open water for an osprey on the hunt.

Watch, too, for a great blue heron in the inlet, standing still as it watches for frogs and fish in the shallow waters.

The walk to Ferry Farm site and back is 2.0 miles.

Round Barn is a remote, quiet spot, with striking views over Flagstaff Lake and up to the Bigelow Range, and a compelling history. Walk one of these trails on your next visit—or walk them all! Imagine what it was like to live here, work here, have the Bigelow Range as backdrop for everyday life.

Appalachian Trail North to Flagstaff Lake East Cove

Dead River Township

Overview: 1.0 mile out and back walk along a section of the Appalachian Trail (AT) to a gravel beach on the lower east shore of Flagstaff. Long, striking, views westward up the cove, and south over the forest to the Bigelow Range. Little to no elevation gain, on a dirt and leaf litter footpath with occasional rocks and roots, and wet areas crossed by bog bridges. Walk on a section of the AT seldom visited by day trippers!

Trailhead: Appalachian Trail crossing of East Flagstaff Road, 0.5 miles west of junction with Long Falls Dam Road.

From North New Portland, drive north on Long Falls Dam Road 17.5 miles, passing through Lexington Plantation, Highland Plantation, and a corner of Carrabassett Valley. After crossing the town line to enter Dead River Plantation, look for a row of mailboxes on the right and a gravel road angling to the left. This gravel road is East Flagstaff Road. There is a street sign, and a small brown and white sign for Bigelow Preserve. Drive west, passing the Maine Huts and Trails route linking Poplar Hut (south) and Flagstaff Hut (north); the Carriage Road to the left; Bog Brook Road to the right. The Appalachian Trail is within 0.1 mile past Bog Brook Road.

The AT crossing is more readily noticed on the left (south) side of the East Flagstaff Road.

Watch for a brown trail register on a post, and a worn trail marked by white paint blazes on trees.

Opposite, on the right (north) side of the road is a turnoff to a gravel pit and parking area. Leave vehicles here. Walk back a few steps to the East Flagstaff Road. Next, walk in the direction of the Long Falls Dam Road for 100'. Watch for white paint blazes on trees. The AT turns left (north) to head into the woods, ascending a short rise.

Nearest Town: North New Portland. Gas up before driving to this area. Nearest gas at this writing is in Kingfield or Embden. There are no services in or near the Bigelow Preserve. General store and diner in North New

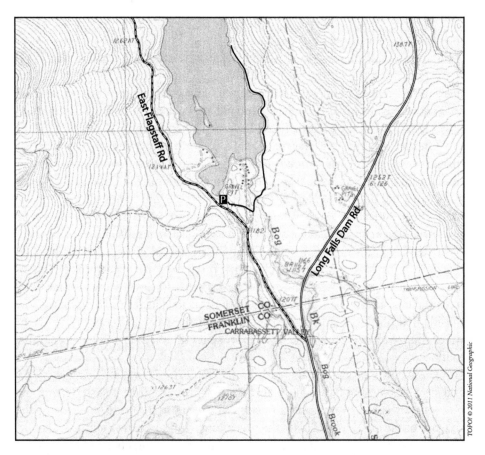

Portland. Seasonal private campground in Lexington, "Happy Horseshoe" has a small store with limited hours.

Maps: Delorme *Maine Atlas* Map #29, 5-C & #30, 1-C (Trail on the ground runs closer to the shore than this map indicates.) Bigelow Preserve Map (Maine Department of Agriculture, Conservation, and Forestry, 207–287–3821, search on line for the above Department and Bigelow Preserve.); *The Valley Below*, map available at High Peaks Information Center, Maine Highway 27, Carrabassett Valley; www.eustismaine.com/thevalleybelow; Maine Huts and Trails System Map; USGS: Little Bigelow Mountain.

Elevation Gain: Negligible

On Trail:

It is a sunny summer morning when I step out on the AT to reach a cobble and sand beach on the southeast cove. I have been here before, when on extended hikes of the Appalachian Trail, and recall this cove with its beach as a remarkable spot—a worthy destination in itself. Today I am back to make it my destination, linger here, take in the pristine lakeside, have a lakeside lunch.

After leaving the East Flagstaff Road I walk up and over a knoll and in 0.1 mile cross the gravel Bog Brook Road. This road leads to the shore of the lake. A remnant of the pre-lake era, it was the state highway route to Dead River homes and farms, and beyond to Flagstaff Village. A few seasonal camps stand along the road within 200 yards of the water, out of sight from the AT crossing. *There is no public parking near the lakeshore, and no parking where the AT crosses this road.*

I head into the woods to pass through the mixed growth so common in this part of the Maine woods: maple, white birch, balsam fir, cedar. Speaking of cedar, bog bridges made of saw-ripped cedar cross low, wet sections that lie in from the lakeshore. The trail emerges from these lowlands to slab along the low hillside that borders the narrow cove. Through-the-trees glimpses of the bright water change to full views as the trail approaches the shore line and runs parallel to it.

These first views are of the cove itself. The water is low, exposing boulders and stretches of sand between the forest rising abruptly from the shore, and the blue-purple waters of the lake, topped by white caps. The wind roars down the lake out of the northwest. This is the prevailing wind on many a summer day—a good tailwind for those paddling down the lake, but a tough headwind for those heading up the lake. Wind-driven "dry-ki"—driftwood—lines the shore, testimony to the prevalence and power of the northwesterlies! No worries for those of us on foot—although that extra layer of warm clothing in the day pack may make the difference between sitting on shore to look at the view, versus huddling out of the wind in the nearby woods.

As I hike northward, just a few feet in from the lake, longer views open to the northwest, beyond the mouth of the cove. The wind roars. Breakers crash on the shore. Quite a sound. Quite a sight.

I reach a tent site for hikers on the AT—my turnaround point. But first—to the beach! A spur trail leads to the shore. No one else is here at mid-day. Most long distance hikers on the AT hike with daylight. They are on-trail at dawn, often hiking until dusk.

Ah, the great wind on my face! Whitecaps glisten in bright sun, trailing white bubbles and froth. Roar, roar! A cedar leans nearly straight-out over the water, offering a bit of a wind break. I sit in its lee on a convenient rock, break out a long-sleeve warm layer and some lunch, and just plain enjoy. Woods, water, wind, sun—here on a half-mile walk from the East Flagstaff Road, at a spot all but unknown to all but those on a long AT trek.

But now *you* know!

Stratton Brook Pond Trail

Wyman Township

Overview: 1.0 miles one-way (2.0 mile round-trip) forest, pond, and brook-side walk over level ground on the south side of the Bigelow Preserve. Distance may be extended by continuing past the outlet to Stratton Brook on the east-bearing route, past the pond, and then parallel to upper Stratton Brook (but out of sight because of thick forest).

Highlights: High peaks views: Sugarloaf, North and South Crocker, Avery Peak, West Peak, and South Horn; Stratton Brook Pond; classic foothills mixed hardwood-softwood; ecological niches—foothill forest, bog, meadow, pond—home to abundant and varied wildflowers and birdlife. Extraordinary variety of views for a lowland trail.

Trailhead: Stratton Brook Pond Road 1.0 mile north of Appalachian Trail (AT) crossing of Maine Highway 27 in Wyman Township. Heading north, watch for large blue sign for Bigelow Preserve. 0.1 mile north of the sign, pass Pond Loop Road on the right. The Stratton Brook Pond Road (blue street sign) is the next right, less than 100 yards farther. Turn right on Stratton Brook Pond Road where there is also a small sign for Bigelow Preserve.

The turn-off from Highway 27 comes up quickly, and signs are small—watch closely for this intersection.

Drive 1.0 mile east on this narrow graveled road to reach trail kiosk and parking area. The road does continue for an additional 0.4 miles to the outlet of Stratton Brook Pond, and a primitive campsite, but the road is rough, often with a large mud pond in the middle. If other parties have driven in there is little space to park or turn around where the road ends at Stratton Brook. (0.4 miles is a long way to back up.)

After walking the 0.4 mile to the outlet of the pond, continue straight (east), crossing Stratton Brook by a planked footbridge.

Nearest Towns: Stratton (north); Carrabassett Valley (south)

Maps: Delorme *Maine Atlas* Map #29, 3-C, D; Maine Huts and Trails Map; *The Valley Below*, Bigelow area map available at High Peaks Information Center, Highway 27, Carrabassett Valley Mountain Bike Trail Map, also available at Information Center; USGS: Sugarloaf Mountain

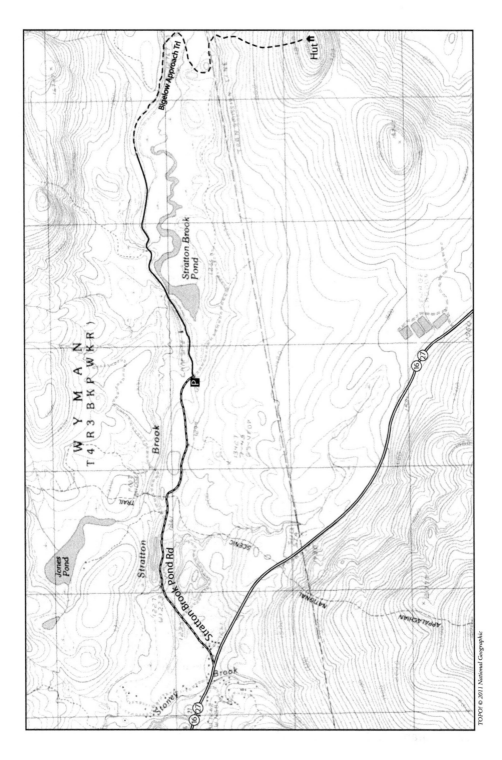

Elevation Gain: negligible

On Trail:

Stratton Brook Pond is a peaceful spot. I come here to start many a hike up to the Bigelow Range, to snowshoe the lowland in winter, and to launch a canoe or kayak for a quiet paddle in summer. Particularly in early spring and in late summer or early fall I come here for a short hike, do some bird-watching, enjoy the rich, angled sunlight of shoulder seasons.

One late summer day I park at the trailhead parking area, shoulder my day pack, and head out for what will become a 2.0 mile out-and-back hike. I am in discovery mode, no hurry. For the first 0.4 mile I hike a balsam fir "tunnel", well-shaded, along a low ridge above the western edge of the pond, which becomes increasingly visible through the trees to the right. At the end of the road stands a rough Bigelow Preserve campsite. No vehicles parked here on this day, but I have come here at other times to find the limited space to park quite full—and glad that I did not drive in myself.

The well-worn pathway drops to a wooden footbridge constructed in 2014, replacing what used to be a rock hop or ford at the outlet of the pond. I enjoy good pond views from the bridge, and more views open up as the trail continues easterly. To the north rise West Peak and Avery Peak, two of the 10 four-thousand foot plus mountains in this High Peaks region.

For a view over the pond, I scramble up the short hill at the far side of the bridge where there is another campsite. For overnighters who seek a breezy site and a good vantage point, this spot may be preferable to the one near the west end of the bridge.

Back on trail I am on essentially level ground, walking east, with the pond on my right. I step toward the pond from time to time to scan the waters, looking upstream where the Brook feeding the pond disappears into acres of broad bog fed by run-off from the Bigelows.

To the south towers Sugarloaf, and to the west rise the twin peaks of North Crocker and South Crocker—all three topping four thousand feet in elevation.

I hike on to a trail divide where the Fire Warden Trail turns 90 degrees to the north. Another Bigelow Preserve campsite stands at this divide. The Stratton Brook Trail continues east, drops into a draw which I cross by rock steps, then ascends to the old road bed once again to continue in an eastward bee-line. Here the trail moves away from the pond and the brook, and passes through stands of thick fir, interspersed with red maple, white birch, and yellow birch. Though another three weeks remains on the summer calendar, some of the maple sport red and orange leaves, sign of the change of seasons to come.

After a half hour of walking, I select a glacial erratic boulder for a turn-around point, and retrace my steps. The trail does continue, known to mountain bikers as the Esker Trail beyond Stratton Brook Pond, eventually to reach the trail junction with the Bigelow Approach Trail, a steep uphill route to Stratton Brook Hut. However, to walk farther would be to enter increasingly remote terrain, most with limited views, and away from my starting point. I am having a fine short walk, and am happy to turn around here.

The day is sunny, breezy, bright. A cacophony of honking overhead announces the flight south of Canada geese, in their distinctive V-formation, flying low over the Maine woods. There will be more such migrating formations in the weeks ahead.

Soon I am pond-side once more, where the waters lie a deep, rich blue. The afternoon sun draws low. A few moments more and I reach the parking area. A fine walk in the woods!

Appalachian Trail 2000 Mile Marker/ Cranberry Stream

Coplin Plantation

Overview: 1.0 mile (2.0 mile round trip) hike over undulating terrain to Cranberry Stream Tent site in the Bigelow Preserve—a possible picnic spot. 100′ beyond the tent site a sign and log bench at an elbow in Cranberry Stream mark the 2000 mile spot. From Springer Mountain in Georgia, southern terminus of the Appalachian Trail, this point is 2000 miles on the trail. One viewpoint towards the Bigelow Range. Footbridge stream crossing. Predominantly a forest walk.

As new AT routes have developed over the years, the 2000 mile point has shifted, and there are other claims to the honor—but this particular spot was determined to be the 2000 mile point in the late 1900s after a period of major trail relocations.

Trailhead: Appalachian Trail crossing of Stratton Brook Pond Road. 1.0 mile east of from Maine Highway 27. This is 0.1 mile past a broad woods road junction on the left. The AT crosses where the road makes a 90 degree turn to the right.

A sign post—minus a sign—stands at the corner. Look for 2–3 parking spaces among the trees on the left side of the road. A sign for the AT with distances listed to various peaks and points of interest, is 100′ up the trail, northbound, but is not easily visible from the road. White paint blazes mark the route but may not be immediately visible from the road. The AT is distinctive as a worn footpath, and should not be difficult to locate once this corner and parking spot is reached. Follow the AT north (left side of the road, driving in).

Alternately—start at the AT crossing of Maine Highway 27 in Wyman Township, where there is a highway sign for the AT, a parking area, and a kiosk with large area maps on either side. Cross the highway, at the north end of the parking area. Follow the AT north 0.9 mile to reach the Stratton Brook Pond Road. *Hiking from this point will result in a hike of 1.9 mile one-way, and 3.8 mile round-trip.*

Nearest Towns: Stratton (north); Carrabassett Valley (south)

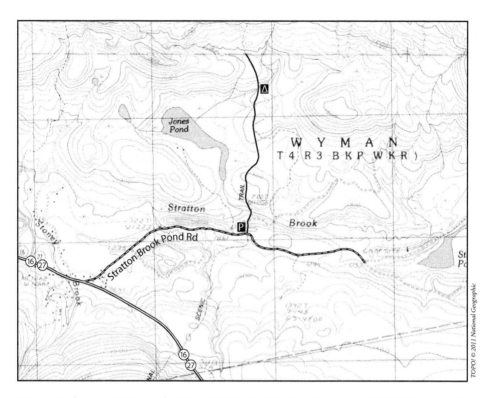

Maps: Delorme *Maine Atlas* Map #29, 3-C; Bigelow Preserve; USGS: Sugarloaf
Mountain

Elevation Gain: 100′

On Trail:

When on one of many hikes I have taken to the heights of the Bigelow Range,
it occurs to me that Cranberry Stream tent site, and the nearby 2000 mile
marker, would make a good short hike. There is a fine view of South Horn near
the start, the bridge crossing of Stratton Brook is a place of interest, particularly
for birdlife and wildflowers characteristic of streamside environments. The trail
offers a good look at classic Maine foothills forest—a mix of hardwoods—maples, birch, ash, beech—and softwoods—pine, fir, spruce, cedar, hemlock. Both
the primitive tent site and the 2000 mile spot itself are places that invite a lunch
stop, or at the very least some lingering and exploring—a good spots to sit, take
in the surrounding forest, hold silence—wait for wildlife to emerge.

I hike on the AT northward, up the rise that divides the Stratton Brook Pond
Road from the brook to the north. At the top of the rise—a quick 40′ eleva-

tion gain—rests a plain log bench, and a clear view of conical South Horn rises against a bright sky. The day is right; the view is clear. On to a descent to the brook, over the bridge, with another pause there. Fish may hide in the shade the bridge affords. I peer into the clear water, but do not see anything. That does not mean that there aren't any fish here at this moment—only that they have chosen this hiding spot well, in the shadow of the bridge.

From this point I walk in a gradual ascent through mixed growth forest to reach the Cranberry Stream tent site. This is a primitive camping area—no picnic tables or fire rings here (no fires allowed, in fact). I sit on a log to enjoy an apple, listen to the twitters and chirps of the surrounding birds. A blue jay complains about my presence. Chickadees and juncos pay me little attention.

On to the 2000 mile marker at a turn of Cranberry Stream. Another sitting spot—this time on a bench constructed for that purpose. I watch the run of the water, the slight riffles, and what leaves or twigs the water bears along. A welcoming spot. What is the rest of the world doing at this moment? In this moment, the world is here, a mountain-fed stream winding down the south slope of the Bigelows, on its way to Stratton Brook, to the South Branch of the Dead River, to the Kennebec River, and, eventually, the sea.

Are you nearby, and wish to hike a mile or two on the AT—perhaps meet a long-distance hiker? Are you simply looking for a quiet walk in the woods? Give this outing a try!

FIELD NOTES

Carrabassett Valley-Kingfield Region

Sugarloaf Mountain, second highest mountain mass in Maine after Mt. Katahdin, is the dominating feature. High snow depth and the configuration of multiple nearby peaks—high and moderate-sized—lead to extensive spring run-off, the carving of river and stream valleys, and formation of many a waterfall. Five waterfalls—the most among the four regions in this book—dot the area, no two alike. The floodplain of the Carrabassett River, and the footpath that follows the former Narrow Gauge Pathway, offer many a waterside walk. The longest outings in this book, the nearly 6.0 mile round-trips to South Poplar Stream Falls and Poplar Stream Falls, are in this section of the book for those who wish to extend their mileage. The other eight waterfall walks or short hikes in this section range from 0.3 miles to 1.4 miles, one way.

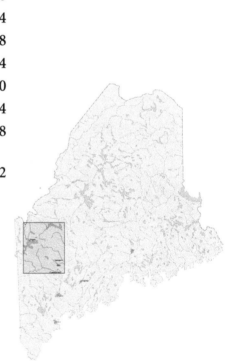

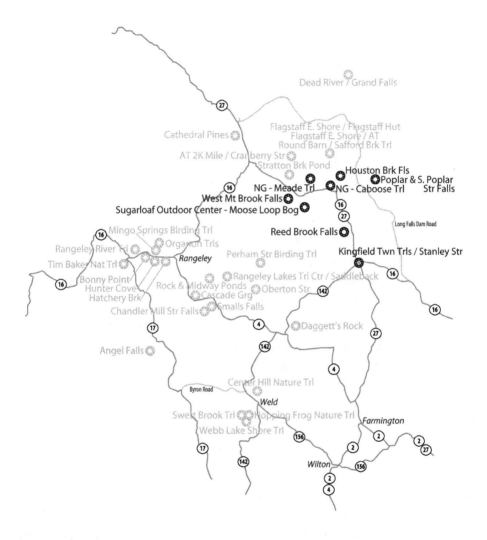

Dead River / Grand Falls

Cathedral Pines

Flagstaff E. Shore / Flagstaff Hut
Flagstaff E. Shore / AT
Round Barn / Safford Brk Trl

AT 2K Mile / Cranberry Str
Stratton Brk Pond

Houston Brk Fls
Poplar & S. Poplar
Str Falls
NG - Meade Trl
NG - Caboose Trl
West Mt Brook Falls
Sugarloaf Outdoor Center - Moose Loop Bog

Long Falls Dam Road

Mingo Springs Birding Trl
Reed Brook Falls

Organon Trls

Rangeley River Trl
Rangeley
Perham Str Birding Trl
Kingfield Twn Trls / Stanley Str

Tim Baker Nat Trl

Rangeley Lakes Trl Ctr / Saddleback

Bonny Point
Hunter Cove
Hatchery Brk
Rock & Midway Ponds
Cascade Grg
Oberton Str
Chandler Mill Str Falls
Smalls Falls

Daggett's Rock

Angel Falls

Byron Road
Center Hill Nature Trl

Weld

Sweet Brook Trl
Hopping Frog Nature Trl
Webb Lake Shore Trl
Farmington

Wilton

West Mountain Falls
Carrabassett Valley

Overview: 0.3 miles one way, 0.6 mile round-trip; series of drops over ledge and boulders, beginning with a 10′ pitch into a chute, 30′ long, carved in ledge, which in turn falls into a broad and deep pool, 20′ wide.

Below the falls lie a series of smaller pools for wading, and flat-top boulders for sitting and sunning. Hike in for the stream view, or to spend the better part of the day enjoying briskly-cold water in the hottest time of summer, or cool, off-brook breezes any day.

Trailhead: Sugarloaf Access Road, then West Mountain Road, following signs for Sugarloaf Golf Course. Trailhead sign is on left, 100 yards before Sugarloaf Golf Course parking area.

Parking for trail is on the right, before the trailhead, just past a stand of maple trees rigged for sapping. Watch out for traffic coming down the road as you cross on foot to reach the trailhead.

Nearest Town: Carrabassett Valley; Sugarloaf Mountain complex

Map: Delorme *Maine Atlas* Map #29, 4-D for Sugarloaf Access Road and Golf Course road. USGS: Sugarloaf Mountain

Sugarloaf Mountain

Elevation gain: less than 50′

On Trail:

On a late summer day, mid-week, I head in to West Mountain Falls as part of a day when I return to some favorite Western Mountains spots for a series of short hikes. The day is bright, and clear. I enjoy a fine view of Little Bigelow Mountain as I drive the last stretch of road before the trailhead parking area.

The trail drops sharply at the edge of the road, moderating as it reaches a junction in under 0.1 mile. Straight ahead a worn route leads to a golf course green, with bunkers visible through the trees. I take a left at this junction. The West Mountain Falls Trail is marked with red paint. At this junction there are two red arrows painted on rocks to confirm the direction.

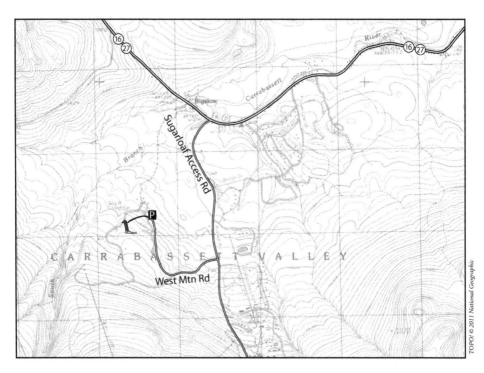

Quite soon I lose sight of the golf course as the trail swings south, curling around a knob to reach West Mountain Brook—which announces itself with a steady roar. The surrounding woods are classic transition forest, with rock maple and white birch mixed with balsam fir, red spruce, and an occasional white pine. Moose maple, with its oversized maple-like leaves, is in abundance trailside.

The trail passes through a small stand of hemlock, drops to more level ground, crosses a wet area over pole bridges, and rises to reach the bank of the brook. Here are the first of many side trails to the water, which is clearly visible to the right. I keep these trails in mind as I head upstream—routes to a picnic point or small wading pool should I seek a quiet spot apart from the more prominent falls above.

The trail tops out by the top of the falls. West Mountain Brook rumbles down a boulder-filled stream, drops 10′ over the first falls, enters a 30′ chute, and drops into a broad pool. I cross ledge to reach the edge of the chute—for a near look at the sheer force of water on the move, water that over the centuries has carved the chute through which it now races.

Although most stream levels are low at this time of the year, West Mountain Falls has a good run of water, fed as it is by the residual of many feet of snow that arrive on high Sugarloaf Mountain in mid-fall and remain late into spring.

The pool below is clear and bright in midday, inviting, but I pass on a dip today. If considering jumping in, be aware that the water is quite cold. As always, inspect for underwater rocks and protruding ledge before entering the water. There is no gravel beach around the pool, but rather a ring of boulders large and small. Water shoes or river sandals would be a good choice to protect the feet!

I pick my way downstream, stepping boulder-to-boulder, aided by my trekking poles. From the top of a massive boulder a lone cedar grows, hovering over a great pool below. Many more cedar grow along both banks. Yet more pools lie below.

After an hour of exploring, and some sitting and listening, just taking all this in—bright day, rush and roar of the falls, spray thrown into the air, swirling waters—I am off to my next adventure. I make my way over to the bank, scramble up to reach the trail, and hike back to the trailhead.

West Mountain Falls is one of the more easily reached waterfalls in the Western Mountains. Spend an hour or spend the day!

Huston Brook Falls

Carrabassett Valley

Overview: 1.4 mile walk (2.8 miles round-trip), mostly on level, graveled road, north of the Carrabassett River, and south of the Bigelow Range. Final 0.1 mile to the falls is a well-worn footpath, which is rocky, and in some places steep, as the route drops down from the high ground near the top of the falls, to reach the beach area and pool below.

Huston Brook Falls is a classic swimming hole. Clear rushing water tumbles down stair-step, bouldered falls, into a broad, deep pool. A small crescent beach lines the nearby shore. Wade in, slip into the waters, and cool off. The brook is fed by cool waters flowing down from the Bigelow Range, and is refreshing even in the height of summer when other lake and pond waters tend to heat up.

The pool is two-pools-in-one. The inner pool, at the base of the falls, is the deeper part. At its outer edge an underwater ledge curves to separate this inner pool from the outer pool, which extends to the beach area. Under most water conditions, there is ample water depth in the outer pool for swimming.

Reach the inner pool on most days simply by swimming over the ledge. There should be plenty of room to spare. My most recent visit to Huston Brook was on a warm mid-summer day. There was plenty of water.

Trailhead: Airport Trailhead for Maine Huts and Trails (Referred to on some maps as "Huston Brook Trailhead") off Maine Highway 27 in Carrabassett Valley. From the south (Kingfield area), travel north on Highway 27 to Carrabassett Valley. Pass the Sugarloaf Airport, which is to the right.

The Trailhead is two driveways past the Airport entrance, on the right, immediately before the "Sugarbowl" indoor recreation center. There is a Maine Huts and Trails sign on the highway, and a Town of Carrabassett Valley sign just in from the turn.

Large parking area has an information kiosk with a map of the Maine Huts and Trails system. Vault toilet on premises.

Nearest Town: Carrabassett Valley

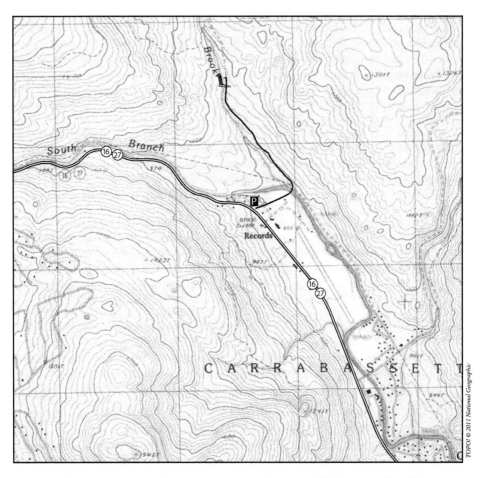

Maps: Delorme *Maine Atlas* #29, 5-C; Carrabassett Valley Mountain Biking
Map—This map shows both the Huston Brook Road and the location of
the Falls; USGS: Poplar Mountain

Elevation Gain: <50′

On Trail:

Let's hike. With our Chocolate Labrador "Moose" as my companion on leash, I
head out from the corner of the parking lot, northeastward across the broad
field at the upper end of the airport landing strip. Signs for both Maine Huts
and Trails, and for the snowmobile trail which follows this first section, point the
way. A worn 2-wheel track also marks the route.

How about this view! The great Bigelow Range commands the horizon. West Peak (4145') and Avery Peak (4088') are the highest summits on the Range. These are two of the ten Four Thousand Footers that cause this area to be known as the High Peaks Region of Maine. To the right of Avery Peak rises the block-like Little Bigelow Mountain, separated from its higher neighbors by Safford Notch. A panoramic view to start this waterfall hike!

In 0.25 miles, I cross a bridge over the Carrabassett River to reach a 5-way intersection for the Narrow Gauge Pathway, Maine Huts and Trails route to Poplar Hut, and the Houston Brook Road. The Houston Brook Road angles left and would be hard to miss with its gravel surface.

The Narrow Gauge Pathway in its upstream direction is blocked to vehicular traffic by a gate and is clearly marked. The Pathway in this direction is a route to the Stratton Brook Hut of MHT and associated hiking trails. (For description of these trails, see *Day Hiking in the Western Mountain of Maine, Second Edition,* 2015.)

Another indication that I am on the Huston Brook Trail is the first of two MHT signs stating that this is *not* the route to Stratton Brook Hut. In 200' pass a 1.0 mile marker on the left. This distance is measured from near the Carriage Road in Carrabassett Valley—you have not yet walked a mile! Nothing fancy about this marker—a small horizontal strip of wood bears the number 1.

The mixed-growth along the road offers shade on a warm day. Sugar maples, ash, and white birch mix in with white pine and cedar. Wildflowers, in profusion, line the roadway—brown-eyed Susans, daisies, and the first flowering goldenrod of the summer. Ahead, framed by the break in the trees, rises the Bigelow Range. Huston Brook rushes about 50' to my left, parallel to the road.

A small turn-out at 0.4 miles on the Huston Brook Road borders a faint path leading into the woods towards the brook. *This is far too soon for the falls, and is not the route!* I keep going.

The road rises, and at 1.0 miles as it makes one final rise, the side trail to Huston Brook Falls diverges to the left. There is no sign. The trail is a well-worn woods path.

(Beyond this turn-off the Huston Brook Road continues, reaches the 2.0 mile road marker in 100', then forks with one gravel road turning west and descending, the other heading more northerly—straight ahead. Reach either of these points, the 2.0 mile marker, or the fork, and *you have passed the turn-off to the falls.*)

The short trail to the falls is well-shaded. It reaches a ledge bluff above the brook, in less than one minute of walking. The trail turns abruptly to the left to descend steeply to the beach, which is visible below. To reach the beach from the road takes me no more than 3 minutes.

Now the fun begins. Anticipating a rocky bottom, I packed water sandals. On some outings, to save weight I pack a spare pair of socks. The pair I wear hiking serve as my water shoes. After my swim I change into dry socks. In I go, swimming across the pool. Invigorating! Our dog "Moose" has a swim too. Refreshingly cooled, I step out of the water for a snack break—then return for a second dip. Moose enjoys the customary "fetch" routine, as I hurl stick after stick into the pool. I tire of the game well before she does.

It is hot enough this day that I do not need a towel. I dry off in the sun. All the while Huston Brook roars its way down the falls, sending broad ripples across the pool. Above, tower high white pine and hemlock, and above these, a puffy-cloud-marked blue summer sky.

On the way out I meet mountain bikers on the road, but Moose and I are the only foot travelers on this mid-summer day. We have enjoyed a private pool! Even with pauses to inspect wildflowers, and check out game trails leading towards the brook, we return to the trailhead in 30 minutes.

Who is next into the pool?

Reed Brook Falls

Kingfield

Overview: 0.8 mile hike (1.6 miles round-trip) on stream-side trail to 20′ wide and 30′ high waterfall on Reed Brook, which drains Shiloh Pond. One of the lesser known falls in the region, even though readily accessed from Maine Highway 27 north of downtown Kingfield.

Trailhead: From downtown Kingfield (Highway 16/27 intersection) drive north on Highway 27 for 3.8 miles. Watch for a gravel turnout on the right, providing fishing access to the Carrabassett River.

This turn-out is immediately before guardrails on both sides of the road that mark the underpassage of Reed Brook. On the left-hand side of the road is the entrance to a log landing. Do not enter the logging area.

For those traveling from Carrabassett Valley, the above turn-out and guard rails are ca. 1.3 miles south of the Kingfield town line with Carrabassett Valley, on Highway 27.

Park at the turnout. Walk westward across the road and approach the guardrail. Before the guardrail look for a pathway heading west into the woods, paralleling the brook. *There is no trail sign but the trail is well cut-out.*

The trail stays on the near side of the brook throughout its length.

Nearest Town: Kingfield

Maps: Delorme *Maine Atlas* Map #29, 5-D indicates Reed Brook and its crossing under Highway 27; USGS: Kingfield

Elevation Gain: ca. 50′

On Trail:

My most recent hike is on a bright, late spring day when a good run of water tumbles down Reed Brook to pass under Highway 27 and flow into the Carrabassett River. After parking at the turn-out on the river side of the highway, I cross the road to enter the trail by the near (south) end of the guardrail.

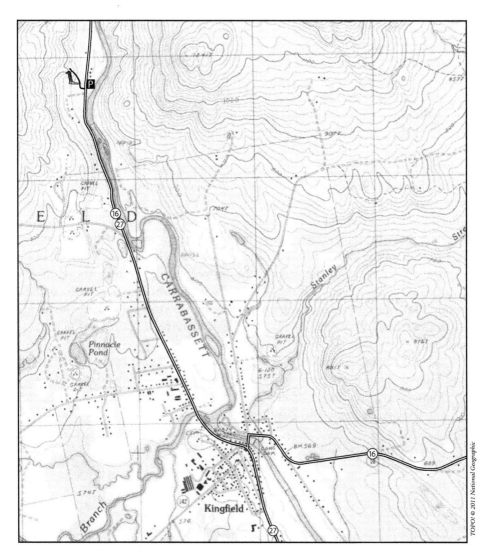

No trail sign or markers, but the path is clearly evident. Reed Brook is clearly visible to the right of the trail.

In 5 minutes I pass a series of pools—deep enough on this day to splash in if I choose, but my destination is the falls themselves. Reed Brook rattles over its stony bed. The air is cool in the shade of a mix of hardwoods and softwoods, with great hemlock, up to 2 feet in diameter, predominating.

Recent trail work has moved the route away from the stream bank, to protect the bank and the trail, and thereby curb erosion. Rope barriers and footbridges across hillside draws are among the features—and give the hiker assurance that this is a maintained trail.

In 0.4 mile the trail passes the edge of a recent timber harvest, and at 0.5 begins to ascend steadily. What was once a path in the forest becomes the rocky way common to many Maine hiking trails. I clamber over one massive, fallen hemlock, and under another. Then I hear the low roar of the falls, peer through the growth ahead, and see rivulets bright white in the morning sun.

A bit more ascent, and I pass a great midstream boulder—at the right water level perhaps a good spot for lunch. One more hemlock to clamber over, and I am soon at the base of the falls.

The falls stand as a broad, 20' wide near-vertical slab, that I estimate to be 30' high. The waters separate into a set of courses, each falling in its own pattern, some narrow, some wide, some slide gently down the slab, others splash noisily after a few feet of free fall.

The water is high enough today that there are two pools at the base of the falls, one on either side. Of the two, the one to the right as I face the falls, is the deeper. Not a large pool, but more bathtub sized, it might offer a cool dunk on a hot day. The rocks can be quite slippery here and trekking poles can come in handy. I settle for the near side, maneuvering my way to a spot where the falling waters splash onto my open hands, and I toss the refreshing drops onto my face and hair.

A lunch break on a stream-side rock, one more moment by the falls to watch and listen to its pleasing rush, and I make the return hike to the trailhead.

Quite a surprise this waterfall—a few minutes of hiking from busy Highway 27, and few people know that it is there!

South Poplar Stream Falls

Maine Huts and Trails
Carrabassett Valley

*N*ote: This entry describes a counter-clockwise ascent by Larry's Trail to South Poplar Stream Falls first. I add information about continuing to Poplar Stream Falls and return towards the trailhead via Warren's Trail.

In the chapter following this one for Poplar Stream Falls, I provide the opposite, clockwise, route. First to Poplar Stream Falls by Warren's Trail, then on to South Poplar Stream Falls and a return by Larry's Trail.

Poplar Stream Falls (24' drop) and South Poplar Stream Falls (51' drop) are two separate horsetail waterfalls, located 0.2 miles apart, on separate streams. Separate trails provide the most direct route to each: Larry's Trail to South Poplar Stream Falls; and Warren's Trail to Poplar Stream Falls (described herein). A 0.2 mile connecting trail provides access from one to the other.

Hikers may hike a loop that includes both sets of falls, using either Larry's Trail to South Poplar Stream Falls as the approach, and Warren's Trail from Poplar Stream Falls for the return; or vice versa, visiting Poplar Stream Falls first, by Warren's Trail, then continuing to South Poplar Stream Falls to return via Larry's Trail.

I tend to visit South Poplar Stream Falls, by Larry's Trail, first; hike the 0.2 miles over to Poplar Stream Falls, and return via Warren's Trail. But often I make these South Falls my final destination, approaching by Larry's Trail, returning by Larry's Trail. This means I may forego Poplar Stream Falls entirely, on some outings.

How come? Both sets of falls are impressive. I find the small floodplain and natural amphitheater by the South Falls a compelling spot to take an extended break. Many sitting rocks, fine face-on view of the falls, quite a chorus of tumbling water. A thunderous and response echoes back and forth across this pristine setting—natural stereo. Works for me! To be sure, I enjoy Poplar Stream Falls, and have been there many times, and in all four seasons.

What this discourse means is that you have choices!

A side trip to Poplar Hut of Maine Huts and Trails will add up to 1.2 miles round-trip to the hike.

Overview: 2.8 miles one-way (5.6 miles out-and-back) to 51' high South Poplar Stream Falls on South Poplar Stream, with option to continue to 24' Poplar Stream Falls on Polar Stream proper, 0.2 miles farther. South Falls, a high falls of remarkable beauty plummets into a 60' diameter pool, located in the center of a natural, west-facing amphitheater rimmed by

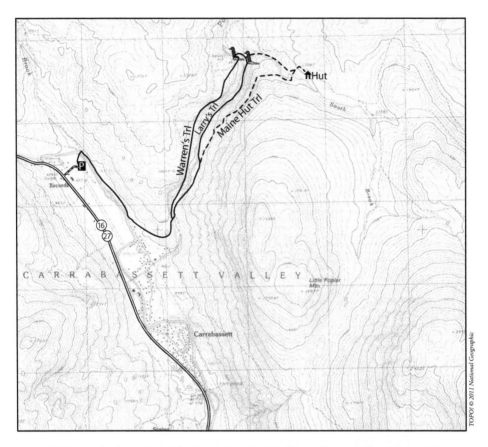

TOPO! © 2011 National Geographic

high hemlock, yellow birch, and cedar. Trails maintained by Maine Huts and Trails.

Optional additional 0.6 mile hike (additional 1.2 miles round-trip) to Poplar Hut of MHT, where lodging and meals are available—services varying with the season. Day visitors welcome.

(MHT: www.mainehuts.org 207–265–2400.)

Note: This is the longest hike in this book, and enters a remote area. I include it for the beauty of both of these high falls, and the generally level approach to the South Falls once the walker reaches Poplar Stream.

Hikers are advised to carry a map, ample water and food, layers of clothing in case of weather changes, a whistle for emergency signaling (cell phone service unreliable), first aid supplies, and a headlamp. As with all waterfalls in this book, water shoes are recommended in the event that someone in the hiking party wishes to enter the pool at the base of the falls. These water shoes should be carried, not worn for hiking. The trail itself is mostly over level to rolling terrain, but in some sections there are rocks and roots on trail.

Trailhead: Airport Trailhead, off Maine Highway 27, 2nd driveway north-bound beyond Sugarloaf Regional Airport, and beside the "Sugarbowl" indoor recreation center and restaurant. For those heading south on Highway 27 from the Sugarloaf Access Road area, or the Sugarloaf Out-door Center, watch for the Sugarbowl on the left when approaching the Airport.

The entrance is signed—both the Town of Carrabassett Valley, and Maine Huts and Trails provide signs. Parking area, vault toilet, and trail kiosk with map display.

To reach the trail to the falls, follow Maine Huts and Trails (MHT) signs towards the Carrabassett River. This connector route is a multi-use route, and appears as a two-track dirt track. After crossing of the river via the William Munzer Memorial Footbridge, the trails separate.

Take the MHT trail towards Poplar Hut, listed here as 3.1 miles. This trail is well-signed, and leads diagonal right.

Nearest Town: Carrabassett Valley in vicinity of Trailhead and Sugarloaf Regional Airport

Maps: Delorme *Maine Atlas* Map #29 5-C (Map lists place name "Records" rarely used locally); Maine Huts and Trails System Map, usually available at trailhead kiosk; also at Maine Huts and Trails Office, Kingfield; USGS: Poplar Mountain

Elevation Gain: Trailhead to South Poplar Stream Falls 200'. There is a sepa-rate gain/loss of 50-100' between the trailhead and Poplar Stream at the Carriage Road.

On Trail:

I check my gear: Trail map, compass, whistle, camera, 1 liter water bottle; lunch with apples and mixed nuts as extra; rain/wind shell, long-sleeve underwear top (packed); knife, first aid kit, emergency "space" blanket, headlamp. The day is cool, bright—a great day. I cover the 0.2 miles of connector trail from airport trailhead to the river, have a look and listen at the noisy Carrabassett River, and take the MHT route towards Poplar Hut.

At first the trail parallels the Narrow Gauge railway bed below and to my right, and I have views of the river through the trees. In fewer than 10 minutes the trail veers left (north) away from the river, to arc around the end of a low ridge separating the valley of the Carrabassett River from that of Poplar Stream. As I round the end of the ridge I gain a view of Poplar Mountain through the trees. The trail drops to the gravel Carriage Road, crosses, and approaches a new bridge over Poplar Stream. I reach the Carriage Road after 30 minutes of hiking from the Airport Trailhead. For a hike to the South Falls and back, my major elevation gain is now behind me—until I come back to this point when I return. From here to the South Falls, the trail lies on level to gradually rising ground.

There is no parking at this road crossing. This is private property. Kindly respect landowners to preserve trail passage.

Immediately before the bridge, on the left after the road crossing, stands a sign for Warren's Trail. This trail runs along the near bank of Poplar Stream, ascending 1.6 miles to Poplar Stream Falls—which are a *separate set of falls* from those on South Poplar Stream. See the next article for a description of how to hike a loop that includes both sets of waterfalls.

Beyond the bridge, the trail, 12' wide and grassy, bears left. In 0.1 mile it passes a junction with the abandoned side trail leading over a short and steep hill to descend to the Gauge Road, and a former MHT trailhead. A sign here indicated that the trail is no longer maintained. I continue on the main MHT trail over mostly level ground, before making a short ascent to gain the high bank on this side of Poplar Stream.

A total of 1 hour of hiking brings me to the side trail to South Poplar Stream Falls, marked on a trail sign as a "snowshoe trail". I turn left here, following a trail that is a bit narrower than the main MHT trail, but fairly level, over what appears to be a an old woods road. The trail bed is mostly soft dirt and leaf litter—not bad in the land of rocks and roots! Poplar Stream rushes by to my left, 50–75' away. The firs, maples, and birches shade the trail, and a light, cooling breeze works its way down the stream valley. Good hiking conditions.

Evidence of sound trail work here. Water bars of stone direct water away from the trail. Split cedar bridges and rock steps keep boots out of mud and water, or from eroding the trail. Thank the MHT and many volunteers for this work! I reach a cedar footbridge with railing, raised 8' above the water to survive high water at spring run-off. This bridge spans South Poplar Stream—and I hear the roar of the falls rises, a distinctly different song from that of nearby Poplar Stream.

I cross the bridge, follow the trail over a small, forested floodplain—and spy the falling waters through the trees. Only a few more steps, and I am in the amphitheater, falls in the center, a lacy, rushing, tumbling spray, dropping into a broad pool. Waters exiting the pool gurgle and rush with their own sound. All this echoes in the amphitheater. Cacophony! Such a sound! Such a place!

Lunch time. Watch time. Listen time.

I spend a half hour here, after a hike in of 1.5 hours. That is 2 hours total. Turning around here, retracing my steps, would return me to the Airport Trailhead in 1.5 hours, for a total outing of 3.5 hours. I note the time of day, and the

hour of sunset. To be back at the trailhead by sunset—darkness comes early in the valleys among mountains—I should have 4 more hours.

Many a time I have turned around at this point. Other days I have hiked on to the hut for a look-see, chat with the crew, maybe buy a cup of tea when the hot water is on. On some days I have hiked on to the other falls—Poplar Stream Falls on Poplar Stream itself. Be aware of the time of day, the energy level in a hiking party, weather, and food and water supplies before hiking farther away from the trailhead.

South Poplar Stream Falls are a worthy destination unto themselves. Enjoy!

For those hiking to Poplar Stream Falls: Continue northward on Larry's Trail, climbing out of the amphitheater up 80 rock steps to reach a trail junction (signed). Here one trail goes straight, to lead to Poplar Hut; and the route to Poplar Stream Falls is a 90 degree turn to the left.

The trail to the falls descends sharply over rocks and roots to reach a steep spur trail dropping down to the pool below Poplar Stream Falls, and a face-on view of the 40′ falls as they drop over ledge, and down a rock chute. Beyond this spur the trail ascends less steeply to a service road, turns left, and crosses Poplar Stream just above the lip of the falls by a vehicle bridge. At the end of the bridge is the junction with Warren's Trail, which offers a route back to the Carriage Road crossing, and to the Airport Trailhead. (See the next entry for more information about Warren's Trail.)

Poplar Stream Falls

Carrabassett Valley

*N*ote: This entry describes a clockwise ascent by Warren's Trail to 24′ Poplar Stream Falls first. I add information about continuing to South Poplar Stream Falls and the return towards the trailhead via Larry's Trail.

In the chapter previous to this one, I provide the opposite, counter-clockwise, route. First to South Poplar Stream Falls by Larry's Trail, then on to Poplar Stream Falls and a return by Warren's Trail.

As I note in the previous chapter, this hike is the longest in the book, at 6.0 miles round-trip. See my comments in the South Poplar Stream Falls entry regarding trip planning, gear, food, water and safety considerations for a hike of this length.

Overview: 3.0 mile one-way (6.0 mile round-trip) by Warren's Trail, to a two-step "horsetail" falls. The first drop is 24′ into a broad pool. Below this pool is a second drop of 12–15′ into a smaller pool. Because of the narrowness of the stream gorge and the location of spur trail that lead to the pool, hikers may miss seeing the lower drop and pool unless looking for it.

If hiking on to South Poplar Stream Falls as part of this outing, hiking a short stretch of Larry's Trail to reach the South Falls, and continuing on Larry's Trail when hiking back towards Airport Trailhead, the total distance is the same—6.0 miles.

Trailhead for Poplar Falls is the same as for South Poplar Stream Falls—the Airport Trailhead. The approach route continues on the Maine Huts and Trails main trail in the direction of Poplar Hut. At the Carriage Road Crossing, Warren's Trail is a left turn before the Poplar Stream bridge. This trail junction is well-signed.

Note: Poplar Stream Falls, and South Poplar Stream Falls are two separate waterfalls, located 0.2 miles apart, on separate streams. There are separate trails that provide the most direct route to each: Larry's Trail to South Poplar Stream Falls; and Warren's Trail to Poplar Stream Falls. A 0.2 mile connecting trail provides access from one to the other.

What's the difference? The two different trails—Warren's Trail along the west bank of Poplar Stream, and Larry's Trail along the east bank—afford some variety in terrain. Warren's Trail passes along Poplar

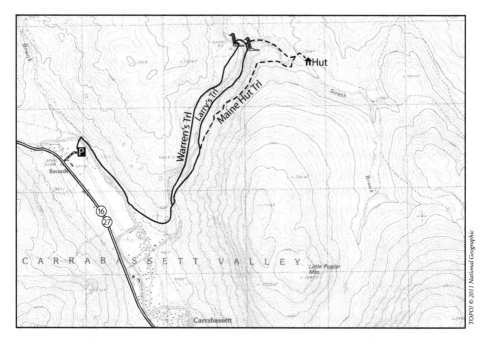

Stream for nearly 1.0 mile, then climbs away from the water to pass along the crest of a high bluff above the stream and out of sight of it, for the remaining 0.6 miles. In the final 0.1 mile the trail returns to border the stream, passing a short rocky spur path downhill to the pool below the falls. The spur offers a fine, nearly face-on view of the falls.

Above that point the trail reaches a service road, turns 90 degrees to the right (east) and reaches the top of Poplar Stream Falls, crosses at a service road vehicle bridge. The trail takes a 90 degree turn to the right (south) leaving the road. The trail slabs hillside on rocky trail for 0.1 mile, passing another short and steep spur trail down to the pool below the falls. This spur lands the hiker directly across from the spur trail reached while hiking up Warren's Trail, and provides another near face-on view of the plunging waters of this 40' falls.

Back on the main trail, the route continues for 0.1 mile more, to a junction with Larry's Trail. Turn right (south) to descend 80 rock steps into the amphitheater at South Poplar Stream Falls. Continue south on Larry's Trail to return to the Carriage Road crossing, and eventually to the Airport Trailhead.

When I hike to both falls I usually approach by Larry's Trail, stopping first at the South Falls. Next I hike over to Poplar Stream Falls, cross the service road bridge that spans the stream immediately above the falls, and return by Warren's Trail.

Trailhead: (Same as for South Poplar Stream Falls) Airport Trailhead, off Maine Highway 27, 2nd driveway northbound beyond Sugarloaf Regional Airport, and beside the "Sugarbowl" indoor recreation center and restaurant. For those heading south on Highway 27 from the Sugarloaf Access Road area, or the Sugarloaf Outdoor Center, watch for the Sugarbowl on the left when approaching the Airport.

The entrance is signed—both the Town of Carrabassett Valley, and Maine Huts and Trails provide signs. Parking area, vault toilet, and trail kiosk with map display.

To reach the trail to the falls, follow Maine Huts and Trails (MHT) signs towards the Carrabassett River. This connector route is a multi-use route, and appears as a two-track dirt track. After crossing of the river via the William Munzer Memorial Footbridge, the trails separate.

Take the MHT trail towards Poplar Hut, listed here as 3.1 miles. This trail is well-signed, and leads diagonal right. Hike around the south end of the small ridge, drop down to the Carriage Road; cross and come to a wide bridge over Poplar Stream. Turn left on Warren's Trail to access Poplar Stream Falls. Continue straight over the bridge for 0.4 miles to reach a junction with Larry's Trail to South Poplar Stream Falls.

Nearest Town: Carrabassett Valley in vicinity of Trailhead and Sugarloaf Regional Airport

Maps: Delorme *Maine Atlas* Map #29 5-C (Map lists place name "Records" rarely used locally); Maine Huts and Trails System Map, usually available at trailhead kiosk; also at Maine Huts and Trails Office, Kingfield; USGS: Poplar Mountain

Elevation Gain: Trailhead to Poplar Stream Falls 300'. There is a separate gain/loss of 50-100 feet between the trailhead and Poplar Stream at the Carriage Road.

On Trail:

I describe a clockwise loop that begins with Warren's Trail to Poplar Stream Falls. Warren's Trail diverges left from the Maine Huts and Trails route to Poplar Hut, at the near end of the Poplar Stream Bridge, immediately after the

Carriage Road Crossing. I begin with a short ascent to high ground along the stream, continuing upstream within 30' of the water.

In 0.1 mile I reach a point where the trail skirts the Carriage Road but does not cross it, re-enters the woods, and continues parallel with the stream, and above it, for another 0.9 miles. At this point the trail climbs, taking advantage of some rock steps built by dedicated trail crew—steps that control erosion—and stone waterbars, which serve a similar purpose by getting water away from the trail bed in a controlled manner. I remind myself to look back, down the valley of Poplar Stream from time to time. It is a clear and bright fall day, after most hardwoods have dropped their leaves. What I look for is a view—and I have it, of 3609' Burnt Mountain.

Viewed down this gap, Burnt looms large, with its close and much higher neighbor, Sugarloaf, hidden from view. For those seeking a moderately steep hike to an open summit, Burnt is a fine hike, offering a look up and down Carrabassett Valley, to the full expanse of the Bigelow Range, and, of course, of the east face of Sugarloaf. I describe the Burnt Mountain hike in *Day Hiking in the Western Mountains of Maine*.

Poplar Stream is but a murmur now, out of sight, far below to my right. My ascent tapers as I near the falls, and I hear the tumbling waters well before I see them. The trail and stream converge, as I reach a side trail dropping down to the edge of the pool below the falls. I scramble down, using care on rock that is nearly always in shade, and often quite slippery. The falls thunder in their nearly two-and-a-half-story drop! I work my way along the outer edge of the pool, along the rocks. The approach to the pool is bit more difficult for this falls than at South Poplar Stream because of the uneven jumble of rocks. My trekking poles come in handy.

A discovery! Below these main falls and the broad pool—which I estimate to be 80' feet across—there is a second falls, smaller with a drop of 12–15 feet, but a falls nevertheless. If the day was a warmer one, I might explore its pool, but not so on this fall day. I am content with the first falls, as I usually am with waterfalls, to sit, listen, watch how the braids of water change direction, or expand and shrink as the volume of water varies from moment to moment. Quite the show!

I hike the remaining few yards to the service road bridge above the falls, select a good sitting rock, and break out my lunch. The falls are but a few feet away, providing as fine a lunch hour background music as I have ever heard.

Some days, this is my destination, and I return by retracing my steps along Warren's Trail. On other days I continue on to South Poplar Stream Falls for a waterfalls double feature, returning toward the trailhead by Larry's Trail. And—as noted earlier, sometimes I approach Poplar Stream Falls by hiking to the South Falls first. No wrong choices here—instead, many options, all good.

One set of falls or two? Out and back, or loop hike? Your choice!

FIELD NOTES

Sugarloaf Outdoor Center
Moose Bog Loop
Carrabassett Valley

Overview: 1.0 mile loop circling Moose Bog, a multi-acre pond edged by bog, at the foot of Sugarloaf Mountain. Essentially level 12' wide pathway over a route groomed for cross-country skiing, open outside of winter season for 3-season hiking, running, and mountain biking. Fine views across the pond from many outlooks. Classic "Oh my gosh!" look to the north face of Sugarloaf from the south shore. Part of a 90 km trail network with many other hiking options.

Trailhead: Sugarloaf Outdoor Center (SOC) Road located on Maine Highway 27, a right turn 1.0 mile south of the Sugarloaf Access Road, and a left turn 0.2 miles north of the right-hand turn to Campbell Field Trailhead.

Once on the SOC road, pass Adaptive Outdoor Center on left at 0.2 miles, and reach SOC parking areas at 0.4 miles. Turn right into the first parking area, where signs point to "Fly Fishing". Moose Loop is Trail 7, marked by a sign with green circle and a 7. The sign also reads "Dillers Loop". This is the correct trail—there are different names assigned to the same trail for winter and 3-season use. This is the Moose Loop!

Walk down the wide path in the direction of the pond, which quickly comes into view on the left, and you are on your way.

The SOC lodge is usually open on weekends July 4 through Columbus Day, with occasional week-day staffing. An information center, toilets, and vending machine are available inside when the facility is open. Portable toilet available in summer and early fall, near the parking area.

Nearest Town: Carrabassett Valley. Gas and groceries available northbound on Route 27 near Sugarloaf Access Road; southbound in vicinity of Sugarloaf Airport.

Maps: Delorme *Maine Atlas* Map #29, 4-D; Carrabassett Valley Mountain Biking Map (available at High Peaks Information Center, Route 27, near airport, and at local retail and lodging establishments.); SOC winter trail system map; USGS: Sugarloaf

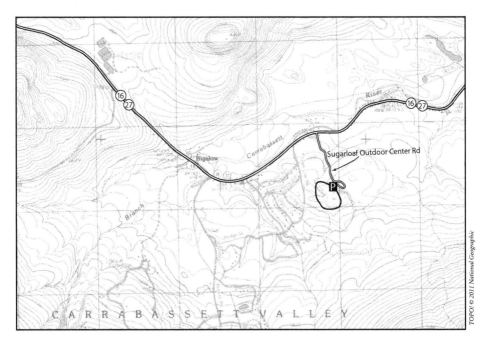

Trail maps are on display at map kiosks adjacent to parking areas.

Elevation Gain: 50′

On Trail:

My most recent Moose Loop hike is on a bright and cloudless November morning. I walk on Trail #7 down the short slope from the parking lot—and the views start from the get-go!

Beside my left extends Moose Bog, where a thin sheen of overnight ice shimmers in the morning sun. Beyond, over high fir and maple, rises the north face of Sugarloaf, fresh snow cover on the high ground. Quite the sight.

Let go of the notion that November is a dreary month! The rich low light of late fall plays on the waters of extensive Moose Bog, shining on glassy, thin ice that has formed overnight. Where there is open water ripples stirred by a light breeze sparkle. Comfortably cool! Great hiking weather!

I cross the earthen dam at the outlet to the bog, step over a rock spillway, ascend a low hill. The trail is grassy, wide—a cross-country ski trail cut to a 12′ width. The walking is fairly easy. Next the trail swings left around a corner near the far end of an arm of the pond, to head east about 30′ away from the water. The bog is multi-colored at this time of year: reds, gold and yellow, orange. The gnawed stump of a young popple (aspen) attests to the work of beaver. This sweet-tasting tree (at least, to beaver, so I am told) is a "hardwood" whose wood is among the softest to be found among deciduous trees. When sawn it does give off a sweet smell.

Northern white cedar and balsam fir, up to 40' high, rim most of the trail, with trailside growth of the same variety standing 2–3 feet tall—the mature, and the up and coming. Other ski trail junctions appear, leading to more of the SOC's 90 kilometers of trail. I continue on trail #7 whenever there is a junction, bog to my left. The trail continues to skirt the bog, then gains and loses some elevation as it climbs a low knoll. Here I meet another hiker coming from the opposite direction. As we greet one another she comments that she walks here almost daily. We resume our respective walks, and another hiker comes my way. This loop is popular enough, but certainly not crowded!

The beaver may be lying low at midday, but not the birds. A pileated wood-pecker works away on the 30' trunk of a dead white birch. Hammering away, looking for a meal, this winter bird pays no mind to me. I stand silently and still, watching, waiting for the woodpecker to move around the tree to enter full-sun. I wait, and wait. There! The distinctive angular head, red crest, black eye bar, red and black stripe leading back from its bill—all this confirms the identification. That sighting alone is enough to make my day.

The trail ascends away from the bog, then descends, to an intersection with Trail #1, another broad trail, that leads right (south) towards upper terrain in the trail system, and left (north) toward the lodge and parking area. Still on the Moose Bog Loop, Trail #7, I cross #1, and enter the woods where signs point the way to "Trail #1 East". One hundred feet into the woods the trail passes a small bog on the right, over a planked bridge, and ascends to another trail junction, the afore-mentioned 1-East.

I turn left here to reach the lodge, passing the 1 East/1 West junction, to reach Moose Bog once more—and enjoy yet another striking "Oh My Gosh" view of Sugarloaf on the horizon, and the sun-touched waters of the bog close-up. The trail ascends a short slope, passes between lodge and pond, where the iconic view of Sugarloaf opens up yet again, framed by the conifers. The loop ends where I began, at the Fly Fishing parking area.

Make the Moose Loop hike part of a regular routine—or walk it to become familiar with the wider SOC trail system. Well-maintained pathways, good views, and much north woods quiet! Lots to like!

Meade Trail
Carrabassett Valley

Overview: 1.0 mile loop along Carrabassett River, and Narrow Gauge Pathway. Option to extend to 1.5 mile hike by traveling a wider loop. Hike/bike trail, mostly level terrain with short spur trails to the edge of the river. Good choice on a warm summer day, for the cool breeze common to the river-way, or for access to the water itself—but a fine hike any time of day, and at any time of year.

Note: This is both a hiking trail and a mountain bike trail. Bikers are to yield to those on foot, and there is signage to indicate this courtesy. I have met bikers on this and other trails, and without difficulty.

The Meade trail draws its name from a locomotive that worked the former Narrow Gauge Railroad. The Caboose Trail—source of that name obvious—is described in the next entry.

Another trail off the "Gauge", the Sargent Trail, is named for a second locomotive. The Sargent Trail is not described in this book, as the trail distance involved is beyond that of most trails contained here. Once familiar with the area, some hikers may wish to explore Sargent and similar trails that link to the Narrow Gauge.

Longer day hikes incorporating the Narrow Gauge, including access to the Stratton Brook Hut of Maine Huts and Trails, and connecting routes between Stratton Brook Hut and Poplar Hut, may be found in *Day Hiking in the Western Mountains of Maine, Second Edition*, 2016.

Trailhead: Campbell Field Trailhead, off Maine Highway 27, 1.0 mile south of Sugarloaf Access Road, Carrabassett Valley. This trailhead provides access to the Narrow Gauge Pathway, Maine Huts and Trails System, and a number of multi-use trails of the Carrabassett Valley Mountain Biking Association. Signage on Route 27 indicates the turnoff to Campbell Field.

Parking area, vault toilet, and trail kiosk with map display.

To reach the Meade Trail, walk towards the Carrabassett River, and cross the footbridge. The Meade Trail (Bike trail #205) is a right turn at the end of the bridge (sign).

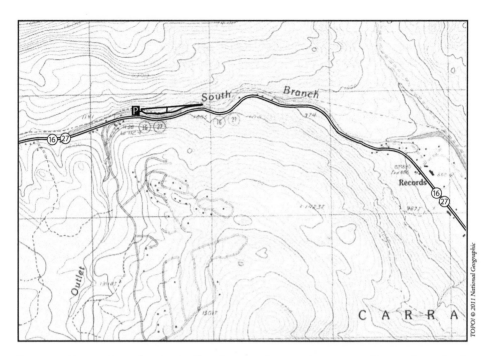

Nearest Town: Carrabassett Valley (Gas and groceries 1.0 north near Sugarloaf Access Road, or 4.0 south in vicinity of Sugarloaf Regional Airport)

Maps: Delorme *Maine Atlas* Map #29 4-C; Carrabassett Valley Mountain Biking Association map (available at Sugarloaf Outdoor Center, High Peaks Information Center south of Sugarloaf Regional Airport Entrance, and at Maine Huts and Trails Office, Kingfield); USGS: Sugarloaf Mountain

Elevation Gain: Negligible

On Trail:

The Carrabassett River runs fast from recent rain as I take my most recent hike on the Meade Trail, on a glowing fall afternoon. The trail runs through forest of northern white cedar, balsam fir, white birch, and rock maple, 30–40' in from the riverbank along most of its length. Rush of the river, waters bouncing off boulders, or raking stream side rocks, delivers background music. From Campbell Field I cross the river by a footbridge, and turn an immediate right on the Meade Trail (Bike Trail #205). In 0.1 mile a spur leads to the edge of the water—offering a spot to linger, have some lunch, or get wet.

Over the next 0.3 mile the route parallels the rivers, as it makes an S-turn where the trail divides.

Straight ahead, in 150', lies the Narrow Gauge Pathway, barely out of sight from the junction. Exiting the Meade Trail at this point, I reach the pathway and turn left, soon to arrive at the Campbell Field Trail junction. Another left turn here and I complete a 1.0-mile loop back to the trailhead and my truck.

On the way I meet another hiker who is headed clockwise around the loop; and one who like I am, goes counterclockwise, passing me when I have stepped to the shore of the river in the early going. I recommend that first-time visitors who plan to hike the shorter loop described above, hike as I have—counterclockwise, entering the Meade Trail immediately after crossing the footbridge, as there is no sign on the Gauge Pathway for the Meade Trail short loop—simply a worn path into the woods.

Taking my time, stepping to the river from time to time, I complete the shorter 1.0 loop in 30 minutes. On other days I have walked the longer loop in 45-50 minutes. Take time to enjoy the Meade Trail—and the rush of the Carrabassett River!

Caboose Trail
Carrabassett Valley

Overview: 1.0 mile loop, with 1.9 mile option, along Carrabassett River, and Narrow Gauge Pathway. Hike/bike trail, mostly level terrain with short spur trails to the edge of the river.

Fine river walk, with return over the well-graded Narrow Gauge.

The Caboose Trail draws its name from the former Narrow Gauge Railway. The rail bed for the railway now serves as a people-powered outdoor trail, open year-round. Hikers, mountain-bikers, cross-country skiers, and those on snowshoes enjoy this riverside and forest route. Note that bikers are to yield to hikers on this trail—but do be alert for those on bikes. Multi-use trails such as Caboose are available because of trail advocacy and construction by the biking community.

The Meade Trail, described in the previous entry, draws its name from a locomotive that worked the former Narrow Gauge Railroad. Once familiar with the area, hikers may wish to explore other hike/bike trails that link to the Narrow Gauge.

Longer day hikes incorporating the Narrow Gauge, including access to the Stratton Brook Hut of Maine Huts and Trails, and connecting routes between Stratton Brook Hut and Poplar Hut, and including Crommett's Overlook, may be found in my book *Day Hiking in the Western Mountains of Maine, Second Edition*, 2016.

Trailhead: Airport Trailhead, off Maine Highway 27, 2nd driveway northbound beyond Sugarloaf Regional Airport, and beside the "Sugarbowl" indoor recreation center and restaurant. For those heading south on Highway 27 from the Sugarloaf Access Road area, or the Sugarloaf Outdoor Center, watch for the Sugarbowl on the left when approaching the Airport.

The entrance is signed—both the Town of Carrabassett Valley, and Maine Huts and Trails provide signs. Parking area, vault toilet, and trail kiosk with map display.

To reach the Caboose Trail, follow Maine Huts and Trails (MHT) signs towards the Carrabassett River. This connector route is a multi-use

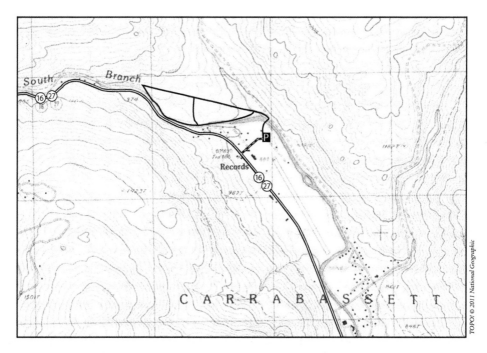

route, and appears as a two-track dirt track. After crossing the river via the William Munzer Memorial Footbridge, the trails separate. The ATV/snowmobile route goes diagonal left over the Huston Brook Road. The Narrow Gauge Pathway (foot traffic) heads 90 degrees left—the direction to Caboose Trail.

Pass through the Narrow Gauge Gate, cross a foot bridge over Huston Brook, and approach a large Narrow Gauge Pathway sign. The Caboose Trail (sign) enters the woods at this point, on the left along the bank of the Carrabassett River.

Nearest Town: Carrabassett Valley—Gas, groceries, and meals in vicinity of Trailhead and Sugarloaf Regional Airport

Maps: Delorme *Maine Atlas* Map #29 5-C (Map lists place name "Records" rarely used locally); Carrabassett Valley Mountain Biking Association map (available at Sugarloaf Outdoor Center, High Peaks Information Center south of Sugarloaf Regional Airport Entrance, and at Maine Huts and Trails Office, Kingfield); USGS: Poplar Mountain

Elevation Gain: Negligible

On Trail:

A n ideal hiking day! I cross the open ground beyond the Sugarloaf Regional Airport, heading towards the Munzer Bridge over the Carrabassett River. Beyond, well above the trees that rim this open area, looms the mountain mass of the Bigelow Range. Center on rises West Peak, and the right of that, Avery Peak, named for early advocate for the Appalachian Trail, Myron Avery, native of Lubec, Maine. Farther right, rises the great wall of Little Bigelow Mountain—hardly little, and so named only by comparison with the higher peaks to its west.

I pause at the bridge. The Carrabassett is low, as is common when summer turns to fall, but noisy, nevertheless. At the far end of the bridge I reach a 5-way intersection: The trailhead connector over which I have walked; the Huston Brook Road, diagonal left; Maine Huts and Trails route to Poplar Stream Falls and Poplar Hut, diagonal right; and the Narrow Gauge rail bed, 90 degree right towards the settlement of Carrabassett Valley and Town Office. A 90 degree turn to the left leads to the Narrow Gauge Pathway and the Caboose Trail.

Sounds complicated, but on the ground it is not. This junction is well signed.

I pass the metal gate that excludes motorized traffic from the Narrow Gauge, cross Huston brook, and immediately come to a large sign for the Narrow Gauge Pathway. Beside it, to the left, a prominent sign reads "The Caboose". Away we go.

The trail parallels the river closely. I enjoy continual water views this day. Plenty of action in the river even at low water. At high water this is virtually another waterfalls hike. Great boulders stand in and along the river. Waters slap and splash, gurgle, roar and rumble. Constant background music!

Impressive tree specimens along the river! I pass through a stand of red oak, two behemoths measuring 4' in diameter; and a great white pine at least 3' across. More—balsam fir, rock maple, white birch, yellow birch, beech.

Under 5 minutes of hiking from the Caboose trailhead, I reach a 30' spur trail to the river and a small cobble and sand beach. I do not pass this up, taking the spur, watch the waters churn and flow, ripple and rush. Back on trail in fewer than 10 minutes total of hiking I come to a draw where the trail takes a sharp right to avoid high water in this streambed—when there is water. I pass more red oak, and an extensive stand of beech, enter an area of short fir and white pine, most under 3' high.

Choice. A trail junction offers an exit straight ahead to the Narrow Gauge Pathway, and a return to the trailhead, for a total walk of about 1.0 mile from the Airport Trailhead.

A left turn crosses the draw, to lead back to the riverbank. My choice. The crossing is an intriguing spot—no bridge, but instead a sloping ledge, acting as a dam, channels the water to a lip narrow enough that I simply step over it. At high water the choice may be to ford (wet feet) or to opt for that shorter loop described above. The trail makes an S-turn, passes a high cedar that leans over the draw, surely nourished by the water that accumulates in a small pool below the ledge.

The trail now heads back towards the river, along the draw, crosses a small draw by a short, planked bridge, and becomes a river walk once again. I pass a group of glacial erratic boulders—always impressive for the glacier force that dragged these huge rocks across the landscape—and one of many massive hemlocks that rise high along the bank.

There are more planked bridges in this section, including one that bridges a large rock in the center of the trail—an advantage of a trail that welcomes both hikers and bikers.

The Caboose ends at the Narrow Gauge Pathway, where I turn right to walk 0.8 along the Pathway to the entrance to the Caboose Trail, where I began my riverside walk. The walking is easy over the Gauge—straight, level, over a well-shaded, tree-lined route. Far down the straight-away I see the Huston Brook bridge which I crossed earlier to reach the Caboose Trail.

Half-way back to the trailhead, I pass the entrance into the woods to the short loop described above. There is no Caboose Trail sign here, but the path is worn—and I see another hiker just coming out from the woods, who has opted for that shorter route.

More straight-a-head walking and I reach the Huston Brook Bridge, exit the Narrow Gauge Pathway, and return to the Munzer Bridge. I pause for a look upstream and down, cross, and make my way back to the Airport Trailhead. A mighty good walk—rushing waters, impressive trees, and a striking view of the Bigelow Range at the beginning and end.

I estimate the longer loop to the farther end of the Caboose Trail to total 1.9 miles; the shorter loop, 1.0 miles, starting and ending at the Airport Trailhead. Time well spent!

Kingfield Town Trails – Stanley Stream

Kingfield

Overview: 0.5 mile loop over forested ground east of the Carrabassett River, and adjacent to Stanley Stream. Inner loops and reversing direction makes longer outings possible. Trailheads walkable from downtown Kingfield (0.2 additional miles). Pleasant forest walk over mostly level ground, with a few knolls and ledge outcrops to cross—and proximity to Stanley Stream along the western edge of the trail network.

Good choice for those staying in town who seek some time on trail without driving a considerable distance. A new trail, with plans to lengthen the route in years to come.

Trailhead: Stanley Avenue, Kingfield, east of Carrabassett River. From downtown Kingfield, cross the Carrabassett River bridge heading east on Highway 16. At the east end of the bridge head straight onto Maple Street, which is a dead-end street. The first right is Stanley Avenue.

Two trail entrances, within 0.1 mile of one another. The *west entrance* on Stanley Avenue coincides with a snowmobile trail (sign for "Lexington"), which heads north into the woods 100′ beyond the Stanley Avenue crossing of Stanley Stream. This trailhead is approximately 100 yards from Maple Street. Limited parking. Please do not block private driveways or block the street itself.

Walk on the graveled snowmobile trail for 100′. The foot trail (also for biking, but no motorized vehicles) is marked with orange flagging, and veers to the right in the vicinity of a maple tapping area, indicated by plastic tubing. Another loop begins 50′ beyond this turn on the left, to lead along Stanley Stream before joining the "maple tap" route. This loop is apparent because trail volunteers have cleared the ground of leaf litter.

The distances on this system are short, and the woods are fairly open, with little undergrowth. I am able to see across the property from one section of trail to the other, over most of the trail system.

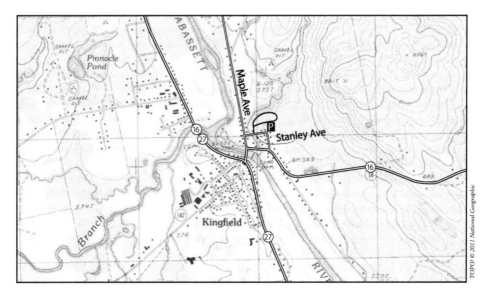

The *east entrance* is at the 90 degree turn on Stanley Avenue 0.1 mile from the west entrance. Here a grassy lane leads diagonal left into the woods. This is a town right-of-way between the yards of two houses.

An orange snowmobile trail sign, and an arrow on yellow backing, mark this corner. Drive 100'. Park on left. This parking area is a snowmobile trailer parking site in winter. The grassed over raised ground ahead is the leach field for the Town of Kingfield. Please do not walk on this field.

The trail, marked with orange flagging crosses this lane adjacent to the parking area. Heading *right* on the trail leads to a short 150' arc that rejoins the grassy lane. Heading *left* leads in the direction of the main trail loop and Stanley Stream.

Total trail distance from end-to-end is 0.5 miles.

Future plans call for designated parking area on or near Highway 16, 0.1 miles from trailhead.

Nearest Town: Kingfield

Maps: Trail map in process of development. Locate Stanley Avenue on Delorme *Maine Atlas* Map #30, 1-E. (Route 16 crossing of the Carrabassett River, and Maple Street are shown on map, but not Stanley Avenue. Note that Stanley Stream *is* on the Delorme map. Trailhead is first right off Maple Street.) ; USGS: Kingfield

Elevation Gain: Negligible

On Trail:

I choose a fall day for this hike, shortly after a period of rain that has brought the first leaf drop to the forest floor. My route will be all-but carpeted, as I make my way along red, orange, russet, and yellow leaves tumbled from the sugar maple and red maple, white birch and popple (aspen), beech and red oak.

I park on the east entrance, in the snowmobile parking area near the town leach field, and walk back 0.1 mile to the west entrance to the trail. The first 100 feet of trail, from the edge of the pavement, is cobble. This turns to grass as I leave an area of backyards and enter the woods on the snowmobile trail that extends towards Lexington, far to the northeast. Stanley Stream, which rises on the slopes of Vose Mountain, flows to my left. After a series of fall rains, replenishing local wells before winter, there is a good stream flow—enough for a few pools to form as waters from the mountains make their run towards the Carrabassett River, the Kennebec River, and, eventually, the sea.

Immediately after I pass a great 4' diameter white pine on my right, the trail, marked by orange flags and tape, turns right, leaving the snowmobile route. I pass momentarily through an area of maple sap collection tubing, leave the sap operation beyond, and am now well on my way.

The heart of the trail system is a winding section that takes in low knolls, steps by rock outcrops, passes by yet another massive rock maple tree—this one 5' in diameter—and crosses a boggy area over a series of 12' wide timber platforms. One loop parallels Stanley Stream. I find the walking to be quite comfortable, and in the course of my outing I walk every section of trail on every loop, and reverse direction, extending my total distance to well over 1.0 mile.

But I am not out for distance, as such. This trail system invites attention to the near view—old stone walls that indicate a time when this forest terrain once was ground cleared for farming, the massive white pines with extensive spreading limbs—another indication of once-cleared land. More near views—glacial erratic rocks and nearby ledge outcrops, the turns and pooling of Stanley Brook, the bog, green with ferns and moss contrasting with the leaf litter from rock maple, popple (aspen), American beech, black ash, cherry standing a few feet away on drier ground. I sit on one good-sized boulder to take in this quiet place apart, marvel at the many expressions of life that surround me.

Walk over from downtown Kingfield—or park by the trailheads. Do have a look at these Kingfield trails.

Plans are to extend this trail, and for it to include high ground with views to the Carrabassett River Valley. Information on the latest trail developments:

Kingfield Town Office: www.kingfieldme.org; kingfieldmaine@gmail.com; 207–265–4637

Weld-Tumbledown Region

Weld has been a hiking destination for generations. Visitors are drawn to hike the many peaks that ring the valley of Webb Lake. Campers and lakeshore visitors often include a hike or forest walk in their plans as they enjoy this striking valley. Mt. Blue State Park offers four short hikes—three of these in the Webb Beach unit of the park, on the west side of Webb Lake, where the campground and swim area are located. The other, east-lying section of the park, the Mt. Blue Unit, offers a short hike on Center Hill, with fine views—spectacular, actually!—over Webb Lake, and towards Mt. Blue and the other high-rising peaks that ring the Weld Valley.

Longer, more rugged hikes to Mt. Blue, the Tumbledown-Jackson Range, Bald Mountain, and Saddleback Wind may be found in *Dayhiking in the Western Mountains of Maine, 2nd edition*, 2016.

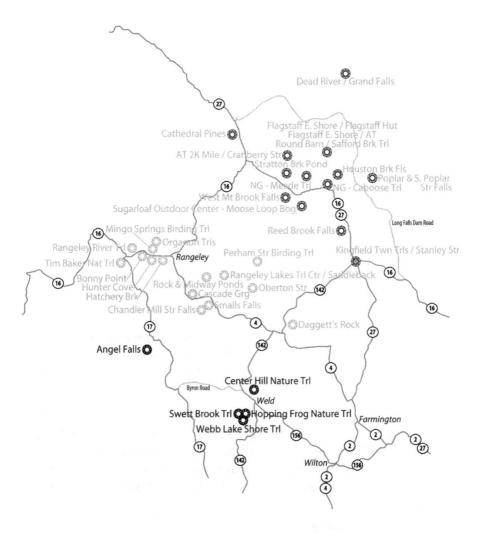

Dead River / Grand Falls

27

Flagstaff E. Shore / Flagstaff Hut
Flagstaff E. Shore / AT
Cathedral Pines
Round Barn / Safford Brk Trl
AT 2K Mile / Cranberry Str
Stratton Brk Pond
Houston Brk Fls
16
NG - Meade Trl
Poplar & S. Poplar
West Mt Brook Falls
NG - Caboose Trl
Str Falls
Sugarloaf Outdoor Center - Moose Loop Bog
16
27
Long Falls Dam Road
Mingo Springs Birding Trl
Reed Brook Falls
16
Orgavon Trls
Rangeley River Trl
Kingfield Twn Trls / Stanley Str
Tim Baker Nat Trl
Rangeley
Perham Str Birding Trl
16
16
Bonny Point /
Rangeley Lakes Trl Ctr / Saddleback
Hunter Cove
Rock & Midway Ponds
Oberton Str
Hatchery Brk
Cascade Grg
142
16
Chandler Mill Str Falls
Smalls Falls
4
Daggett's Rock
27
16
17
142
Angel Falls
4

Center Hill Nature Trl
Weld
Byron Road
Swett Brook Trl
Hopping Frog Nature Trl
Farmington
Webb Lake Shore Trl
156
2
2
27
17
2
156
142
Wilton
2
4

Angel Falls

Township D, South of Rangeley and Oquossoc

See the entry for Angel Falls in the Rangeley-Saddleback section of this book Page 40.

Visitors to the Weld area, including campers at Mt. Blue State Park and other campgrounds and lodgings in Weld, may reach the Angel Falls trailhead without driving first to Rangeley. Driving directions from Weld appear below.

Trailhead: *Directions from Downtown Weld 4-corners:* To reach the Angel Falls trailhead, drive north on Maine Highway 142 from the 4-way intersection in downtown Weld by the Weld General Store. Turn left (west) at Webb Corner/Weld Corner on West Side Road. Drive 0.5 mile to the graveled Byron Notch Road, which proceeds straight ahead, while the paved West Side Road angles to the left. Follow Byron Notch Road to Byron and Maine Highway 17.

Note: There are no services on this road between Weld and Byron. Be alert for vehicles in the vicinity of Tumbledown Mountain trails and for logging trucks all along this road. *Keep to the right.*

From Mt. Blue State Park, Webb Lake Unit camping area: When exiting the park, turn right (north) on the West Side Road. Follow this road to the intersection with the Byron Notch Road. Turn left on the Notch Road.

Once on the Byron Notch Road, drive west past the trailheads for Tumbledown Mountain to the intersection with Maine Highway 17 in the town of Byron. *Note:* There are no services on this road between Weld and Byron. Be alert for vehicles in the vicinity of Tumbledown Mountain trails, and for logging trucks all along this road. *Keep to the right.*

The Byron Notch Road ends just after crossing the Swift River by a bridge at Coos Canyon (rhymes with "choose"). This is a popular summer swim spot—but do take care on slippery rocks.

Note that the Byron Notch Road is not maintained for winter travel between November and May.

Center Hill Nature Trail

Mt. Blue State Park – Mt. Blue Unit
Weld

Overview: 0.4 mile loop trail along the forested east-facing rim of Center Hill, with viewpoints from a broad open ledge, and a series of viewing areas, some with log benches and picnic tables. Trail begins and ends at head of open meadow on Center Hill with long views toward Byron Notch, Tumbledown-Jackson-Blueberry Mountain Range, and Saddleback Mountain near Rangeley.

Varied forest includes pine, spruce, and balsam fir, along with maple, white birch, yellow birch, beech. One small high bog trailside where wild iris bloom in summer. Nature trail flyer available at trailhead.

This short trail is the shortest route in this book offering extensive, and dramatic, mountain views. I recommend it to those new to hiking, and to families with children.

Compared to many mountain trails the Nature Trail is not technically difficult, but there are short steep sections at the very beginning, and at the end, and few long steps to take to reach the open ledge 0.1 mile into the trail. A walking stick or trekking poles may be handy.

Trailhead: Center Hill, in Mt. Blue Unit of Mt. Blue State Park. From downtown Weld four corners, turn east on Center Hill Road, following signs for Mt. Blue. The road swings left (north) and after 0.5 mile ascends to pass an overlook with outstanding views of Webb Lake and the mountains that rim the Weld Valley. Across from the overlook, lie trailheads for separate cross-country skiing, snowshoe, and snowmobile routes; a warming yurt open in winter; and buildings for park vehicles and machinery.

Continue on Center Hill Road, which makes a right turn, and changes in surface from pavement to gravel. At 1.0 mile from this turn, on right, is the Center Hill turn-off—which is paved. Pass through the open gate and past a park building, and 0.4 mile up the hill to the parking area and overlook. The view is dramatic!

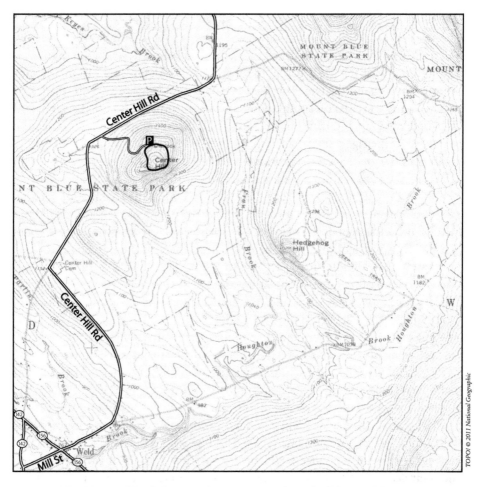

The Nature Trail departs from the south end of the parking area, near the picnic shelter.

A mounted box contains flyers describing stops along the trail. Picnic tables are distributed at many sites along the hill side—and on the Nature Trail. Vault toilet at the north end of the parking area.

The loop trail returns to parking area at the upper reach of the picnic area. While hikers may begin at either end, most start at the marked lower trailhead, as this is the direction for which the trail flyer was written.

Nearest Town: Weld

Elevation Gain: less than 100′

On Trail:

Let us begin with what I see from the picnic area before I even begin to hike! To the west the great gap is Byron Notch, with Old Blue Mountain (not Mount Blue) behind. The Tumbledown-Jackson Range rises on the right (north). Note the cliffs of Tumbledown, the open summit of Little Jackson, and the wooded top of Big Jackson, nearest of the three. Sharp eyes will notice the next peak to the right, the small, bare summit of Blueberry Mountain. Directly north rises the great Saddleback Range, east of Rangeley.

Quite the view—and I have not even hiked yet!

The Nature Trail departs from the southern end of the parking lot, passing a log picnic shelter. For the first stretch, I ascend stone steps, to enter the filtered light of the spruce-fir forest. Notice the spruce tree growing out of the moss that has accumulated on ledge. There is a story there of the persistence of life! The trail swings left and in 100' I come to a short side trail to open ledges with extensive views of the great Weld Valley and Webb Lake. The views here include the range west of Webb Lake, and two almost-twin peaks to the south of Bald Mountain and Saddleback Wind Mountain.

You may want to linger here, take in that view—many views, truly. Imagine the day when so much of the valley below was farmland. People worked the stony ground for generations, until news arrived of deep soil in the Midwest and many farmers left. Some remained to turn to sheep raising and dairy farming. Now much of the land has returned to forest.

I step away from the ledge, to return to the main trail, where more viewpoints await—some with picnic tables, and one with a log bench. A southward view takes in what was once farmland for the early settlers of the Weld Valley, and their descendants. A now abandoned mountain road led from Weld to Temple, across the valley due south of the lookout, passing Mt. Blue to its south, as a shortcut to the County seat of Farmington. I step down a 30' spur for a fine view of Mt. Blue itself, and its junior companion, Little Blue to the left (north) of Mt. Blue.

The trail passes a tiny mountain bog on the left, which in season is bright with iris.

Watch for the occasional hemlock among the spruce and fir, and few white birch—one hardwood that may be found at higher elevations where others, such as maple, beech, and ash, are usually absent. Soon this trail of just under a half-mile brings me to ledge overlooking my starting point, at the parking lot. I could maneuver my way down the ledge, continue down the trail to return to my truck—or reverse direction. My children would beg me to take them back around the trail loop again!

Much to see for a 0.4 mile hike! I have accompanied school groups on this hike, and bring houseguests here. The views are among the finest of all hikes in this book.

Hopping Frog Nature Trail

Mt. Blue State Park – Webb Lake Unit
Weld

Overview: 1.0 mile blue-blazed loop trail over near-lakeshore wetlands through mixed growth hardwood-softwood forest, and by the lower end of Swett Brook, reaching a narrow beach on Webb Lake, and a striking view of Mt. Blue to the west, framed by an opening in the forest. Views extend south to Bald Mountain and Saddleback Wind Mountain; and North towards Blueberry Mountain and the Tumbledown-Jackson Range. Numbered posts along the route are keyed to a Nature Trail interpretive flyer available from Park staff.

State Park entrance fee may apply, depending upon resident status and time of year.

Trailhead: Webb Lake Unit of Mount Blue State Park, on southwest shore of Webb Lake. From downtown Weld four-corners, follow Maine Highway 142 north to Webb/Weld Corner. Turn left onto West Side Road, following signs to Webb Beach and Camping area.

If traveling from Dixfield, take Highway 142 toward Weld, passing through the town of Carthage. Watch for West Side Road at settlement of Berry Mills. Turn left on West Side Road, and follow to the Park entrance.

Enter the Park, stopping at the gatehouse in season. Continue past the gatehouse 0.2 mile to a left-turn towards the Nature Center. The Hopping Frog Trail is across the parking lot from the Center, i.e. I stand with my back to the Nature Center, and the trail is before me across the lot.

A 4″ squared post reads "Nature Trail", inscribed vertically.

From the swimming beach parking lot, the trailhead may be reached by walking from the Webb Beach area by the Shore Trail, or by walking from the campground. Park staff can explain the various routes—and provide the interpretive flyer.

Nearest Town: Weld

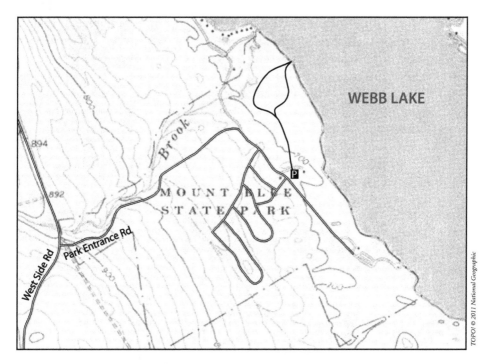

Maps: Delorme *Maine Atlas* Map #19, 2-C; USGS: Mount Blue State Park Map, Maine Bureau of Parks and Lands; USGS: Weld

Elevation Gain: Negligible

On Trail:

On a fall afternoon when sun and clouds mix I step out on the Hopping Frog Nature Trail, to see what discoveries I might make, and to catch a view of Mount Blue and neighboring peaks from the beach lookout point. Once past the trailhead, I enter a forest corridor lined by balsam fir and red maples. The fir predominates—green all around. By my feet ground pine pokes through the leaf litter—displaying yet more green. The pathway is quite smooth here—not many of the rocks and roots commonplace to Maine trails on higher ground. Reason? I walk on old lakebed. The accumulated soil is deeper here than is the case on nearby glacier-scoured hillsides. Hikers who have walked trails in the lowland forest of the American Southeast—Florida, Georgia, for example—may see some similarities in this terrain.

At post #3 the route crosses a low area by cedar bog bridges. This late in the season there is no surrounding standing water, but this section can be damp and muddy in the spring—hence the bridges. Not only do these bridges help to keep feet dry; they also protect the soil from compaction from hundreds of hiking shoes trampling the soft soil. Beyond the bog bridges, at post #4, a 3' wide *bona fide* footbridge crosses a feeder stream that leads to Swett Brook, which itself is out of sight at this point.

This is a rich and varied environment, full of life—good choice for a Nature Trail. Young pine and fir 2–3 feet high share the forest floor with mature trees—and with great pines that have died and are gradually composting into nutrients for future forest.

At 0.3 miles the trail divides for its loop section. A trail sign indicates right for Webb Lake, left for Swett Brook. The choice is not between one or the other, as the loop returns to this point, just a matter of which I choose to see first. I opt for the lake!

After passing a great fallen pine—with a Nature Trail signpost #5—on one side, and a towering twin pine on the other, I enter mixed terrain. A one-span bog bridge, then a leaf-carpeted flat section, and then a true boggy area, where the trail route seeks high places amongst the standing water, and makes use of bog bridges where there is no high ground.

Ta-da! I reach the shore. Wow! The trail opens to an outlook framed by the lakeside forest—a straight-on view of cone-shaped Mount Blue. The great peak rises in the soft light of the late afternoon. Its near-perfect reflection rides on the glassy surface of the lake. All is quiet. I take a seat on a bench, set back 30' from the water, and… Take. It. All. In.

Before I return to the trail, I walk up the beach and discover that beaver have been at work harvesting red maple saplings for winter food supply. Fresh wood chips lie on the ground. Did I interrupt their work? I am reminded that the forests are lively places where wild creatures are busy for food and for materials to build their nests and lodges. When we humans approach, the alarm sounds, and well before we arrive within view, most creatures have disappeared for cover.

Back on trail I continue counter-clockwise, cross yet one more bog bridge, and make my way to Swett Brook. Here another bench awaits, rightly located by a bend in the brook, which forms a 20' broad pool before rattling over rocks to complete the final few hundred feet of forest that lie between this turn and the lakeshore. Another prime spot! I linger here.

The trail rises ever so gradually, reaches drier ground, meets the loop junction where earlier I chose the direction towards Webb Lake, and makes a straight line back towards the Nature Center trailhead. My late afternoon walk, including stops at the lake and at Swett Brook, has taken just under one hour.

I shall hold that lakeshore view of Mount Blue in my mind's eye for quite some time—the dark green cone rising against the eastern sky—and the mountain's mirror image reflected on the still waters of Webb Lake.

Webb Lake Shore Trail

Mount Blue State Park – Webb Lake Unit
Weld

Overview: 1.0 mile north-south trail along the west shore of Webb Lake, bookended by the North and South Shelters, 2 reserve-able group picnic shelters for day use. Fine views east toward Mount Blue across the lake, north toward Blueberry Mountain and the east end of the Tumbledown-Jackson Range, and south towards Bald Mountain. No paint blazes or signage along the route—and the term "Shore Trail" does not appear on any signs in the park. However, the trail is easy to follow, as it is well-worn and runs lakeside throughout its length.

Good opportunities to see mallard ducks and other waterfowl, which nest and raise their young along this stretch of shore which is generally protected from prevailing northwest winds, and where the shallow water discourages power boats.

Trailheads: There are multiple access points: North Picnic Shelter, Nature Center, Webb Beach, Boat Launch, and South Picnic Shelter. Note that most parties will reach the North Shelter by starting at the Nature Center; and the South Shelter is usually reached from the Boat Launch or Webb Beach.

Nature Center: This sits at the end of the Nature Center spur road, 0.2 miles south of the Park gatehouse. A sign for the Nature Center and Amphitheater stands at the entrance to this spur. By the northeast corner of the Center, a trail map is painted on a stone—essentially a "T" shape with a short stem and long crossbar.

The trail descends to the lakeshore. Turn left for the North Shelter. Turn right to reach the sandy swim beach, boat launch, and, eventually, the South Shelter.

Webb Beach: The Shore Trail may be accessed from the swim beach. Turn left, by the lifeguard stand, to cross a small inlet stream over a short foot bridge. Pass the canoe and kayak rental area, and proceed north along the trail, which is 10–20' in from the shore. Proceed to the north end of the trail at the North Shelter.

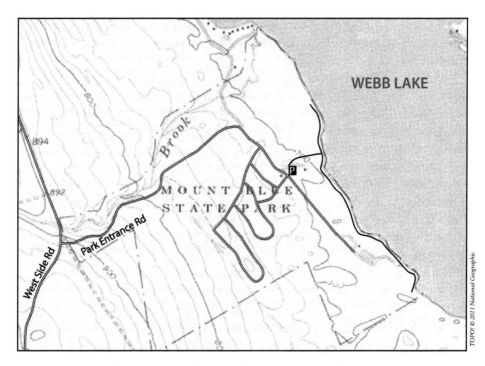

Alternately, turn right by the lifeguard stand, walk along the grass above the sand, parallel to the water. Enter the woods on a distinct footpath. Follow this 0.1 mile to the Boat Launch, and beyond 0.2 mile to the South Shelter.

Boat Launch: The South Shelter is 0.2 mile to the right (south) of the Boat Ramp.

To reach Webb Beach, the North Shelter and/or the Nature Center, head left (north) into the woods on the broad trail that parallels the shore.

Nearest Town: Weld

Maps: Delorme *Maine Atlas* Map #19, 2-C; USGS: Mount Blue State Park Map, Maine Bureau of Parks and Lands; USGS: Weld

Elevation Gain: Negligible

On Trail:

I have walked the Shore Trail on many a visit to Mount Blue State Park, most often when getting in some beach time on the fine sands of Webb Beach or when family camping in the campground located in the Webb Unit of the Park. One afternoon I decide to walk every foot of the Shore Trail, starting from the Nature Center.

From the Center to the lake is a distance of only 50 yards. The short trail ends at a "T" by the lakeshore. I turn left, at this signed junction, in the direction of the North Shelter. Soon I cross an inlet stream over a planked bridge, continue along the leaf-littered path, and step out onto the sand beach for a time, just a few feet away from the trail itself.

The Tumbledown Range commands the north view. Left to right (west to east along the north skyline) run Tumbledown Mountain and the cliffs of Tumbledown, the open summit of Little Jackson, the wooded heights of Big Jackson, and the summit of Blueberry Mountain—a bare summit just a few feet above the surrounding forest. To the east rises prominent, cone-shaped Mt. Blue, topped by a tower. To the left (north) of Mt. Blue is Little Blue. The two peaks on the southern horizon are Bald Mountain with its open ledges, and to its right, the southernmost significant peak in the region, Saddleback Wind. Webb Lake serves as foreground (or fore-water, if that is a word) for all this. In the woods out of which I have stepped, massive white pines, tall and thick, mark the border between forest and lake.

I walk on to the North Shelter, which is empty this day. This is not a surprise for a weekday in the fall. For parties who do not mind hauling their picnic supplies along the trail, this is a great spot for a family outing or a gathering of friends. An option is to launch canoes or kayaks at the boat launch or canoe-kayak rental area, and paddle the gear to the site. With the tall pines, and a-place-apart feel, this is a good location indeed, with its own strip of sandy beach.

Let's turn around to hike south! Back I go, pass the trail junction where the Nature Center spur trail heads back up the rise, and continue along the shore. Shortly before the trail approaches the swim beach, a glacial erratic boulder rests at the water's edge between a mature white pine and a small balsam fir. This is a favorite spot for many people in high summer. When the lake water is high some people fish from this rock. More often this shaded boulder seems to draw kids who simply like to scramble to the top, perch there, and look out across the lake.

The canoe-kayak rental area (simply a strip of sand in the off-season) is next, at the north end of the swim beach. Mallards are a common sight along the shore at either end of the swim beach. They are elsewhere today! Open during the summer season, and located behind the beach, are rest rooms, a changing area, and a water fountain. I continue along the shore, enter the woods again, and follow a broad gravel path to the Boat Ramp. Across the boat ramp approach road the trail again enters the woods, to reach the South Shelter after crossing a short cement bridge over a small inlet stream.

The South Shelter, like the North, is available for rental for picnic purposes by groups.

It sits 100' back from the water. The secluded crescent beach here is idyllic. Our family has come here with friends on many occasions. I have usually been the one designated to ferry provisions by canoe from the Boat Ramp, while others take the short walk. The spot is far enough away from the Boat Ramp and Webb Beach to offer a sense of being a place apart—which it is.

Time to turn around! I head back along the Shore Trail, retrace my steps to the Nature Center trailhead. Walking the entire length of the trail and returning to the entry trail to the Center, is about 1.6 miles—one of the longer lakeshore hikes in the Western Mountains of Maine!

Swett Brook Trail

Mount Blue State Park – Webb Lake Unit
Weld

Overview: 2.0 mile loop trail, a forest walk, crossing Swett Brook twice in the first 0.5 mile, once by a bridge, and once by ford or rock-step. After the brook section, the route ascends westward gradually through mature woods that generations ago were farmland, then turns south to meet the campground-to-beach trail, 0.1 miles from the campground, and 0.2 miles from the swimming beach parking lot.

Trailhead: Lower trailhead is 20 yards north of the park gate (not the gatehouse, but the gate) where there is a small turn-off parking area large enough for two vehicles. If the parking spaces at the trailhead are full, there should be ample room in the parking area by the gatehouse, 100 yards away.

The trail entrance is flagged with blue ribbons. Blue paint blazes on trees mark the trail. I am informed that trail work is planned, and that a trailhead sign may be installed at this point in the future.

Park staff can direct the way to the trail should there be uncertainty.

The route enters the woods, following an old grassy roadway bordered by balsam fir on either side.

High Water Route: One Alternative: The trail crosses Swett Brook twice; first by a bridge; second by a ford, depending upon water level. When water in the brook is high, to avoid the ford, an alternative starting point is 0.4 miles back up the park entrance road in the direction of the West Side Road. Look for a parking pull-out here, and for blue blazes on trees on either side of the road.

Swett Brook is clearly visible on the east side of the road. On the west side of the road, follow the blue-blazed trail, which ascends into the woods. The remaining hike will total 1.9 miles to return to the trailhead after hiking along the west boundary of the park, then south towards the campground, and finally back to the gate and this alternate trailhead.

With this alternative there are no brook crossings, but there is no brookside walking, and the hike is essentially a forest walk.

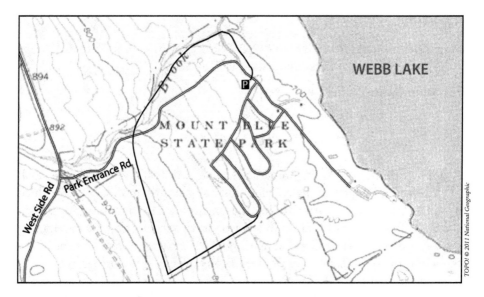

High Water Route; Second Alternative: This route starts at the trailhead by the gate, and follows the Swett Brook Trail over its usual route. It crosses the brook by a fire road bridge, turns left to parallel the brook along the east bank. In 0.4 mile the trail reaches the ford. Turn around to retrace steps, for a 0.8 mile round trip. No wet feet (or more)—and a good stream-side walk.

With this alternative, Swett Brook is nearby for most of the hike.

When hiking the full length of the Swett Brook Trail, note that the trail does not begin and end at the same location. Lower trailhead is near the gate. Upper trailhead is at an intersection with the path connecting the camping area with the swim beach. Returning to the starting point will involve walking through the campground to the gatehouse, then to the gate and trailhead. This campground to gate section adds about 0.4 mile.

Quickly-moving hikers may travel the full 2.0 trail distance, plus through-the-campground route in 1.0 hour, but 1.5 hours may be more of an average—longer with small children. If hiking with small children I suggest planning an out-and-back hike, timing the turn-around to match the stamina of little ones. Or, walk the High Water Second Alternative, which has the attraction of both woods and water. Or, hike the shorter Hopping Frog or Shore Trails (see above). Better to have children say they want a longer hike next time, than to say they never want to go again because the hike was too long!

Unsure? Talk with park staff about terrain and expected time on trail.

Nearest Town: Weld

Maps: Delorme *Maine Atlas* Map #19, 2-C; USGS: Mount Blue State Park Map, Maine Bureau of Parks and Lands; USGS: Weld

Elevation Gain: less than 100'

On Trail:

When I enter the Swett Brook Trail mine is the only vehicle in the small turnout by the park gate. I all but literally plunge into the woods—thick balsam fir, just over head high, line the first 100' of the pathway. Something about the first few steps I take into any woods. I savor entering the envelope of the forest. It is a short envelope, at first, as in 100' I reach a gravel Fire Lane where the trail turns right (sign), crosses Swett Brook over a vehicle bridge, then turns left to re-enter the woods (another sign).

This is classic mixed growth forest—fir and an occasional pine; hardwoods—maple, some red, a few rock; white birch, yellow birch, beech. Bog bridges cross small tributary streams to Swett Brook. I find the going to be fairly easy over level ground padded with decades of leaf drop.

Just as I settle into an easy hiking rhythm—whoa! A ruffed grouse explodes out of the underbrush! Who was more surprised—the grouse or yours truly? The thump! thump! thump! wingbeat fades into the forest. My own heart has taken over the beat! That was a surprise—though surely a pleasant one.

The trail parallels Swett Brook, which is just out of sight for a time, then angles my way to parallel the path. I am hiking on an overgrown lane, barely recognizable as such. Rusted remains of an old truck rest in trailside under-growth—confirming my observation that I am on a old road. What was life like in the day when farmland covered the slopes sweeping up from the west shore of Webb Lake? When the trail meets the brook to cross it, there is yet more evidence of the once-road. Rock cribbing, built from field stones, once the support for a bridge over Swett Brook at this point, lies exposed along the bank.

No bridge today, however! But no need to ford either! The water is low enough to expose rocks for stepping. Deliberately, balancing by my trekking poles, I step rock-to-rock, cross the brook, scramble up the short bank. I spy blue blazes on trees across the road, marking the trail, and continue on my way.

What a fine trail for tree identification—and the study of micro-commu-nities in the forest! Beech and hemlock border an uphill stretch which is dry, and even loamy in spots. Beyond a short wet area, where moss abounds, a beech ridge is next, followed by a hardwood stand of maple, white birch, and popple. Then it is on to a long continuous line of bog bridging crossing more wetland. I pass a thick yellow birch sporting an 18″ diameter burl, sign of an old injury or infestation which the tree has healed by growing a great mass around it. A good friend of mine turns wooden bowls out of such burls, seeing beauty in these ragged, some would say ugly, bulges. A message there.

Along with the blue blazes there are orange blazes, which are markers for an early park boundary. Acreage has since been added to the park, and the orange is simply a reminder of an earlier time. I continue to follow blue trail markers.

The trail takes a sharp left, passing through a break in a stone wall, to head straight east. The turn has no particular marking when approached as I did. I have been hiking along, watching ahead for blue blazes—when suddenly there are no more. Some rust-colored old blazes mark nearby trees, but these are old boundary markers, not trail markers. In such a situation, I stop, scan the woods, look behind me for the most recent blue blaze. Got it—the one behind. A careful scan—and there, off to my left, past the break in the wall, I see a blaze. I make the turn, and away I go.

Hikers coming to this point should watch for twin white birches. The one on the left has a blaze. When I step through the opening in the wall and look back, I see two blue blazes, the top one off-set to the right, indicating a turn. I am on the trail.

On a gradual descent now, heading due east, I hike down through a hard-wood forest with occasional fir and hemlock, enter one more wet area with big bridges, to end finally at the trail that links the campground to the beach. A sign here marks this end of the Swett Brook Trail, and another points in the directions for the campground and swim beach.

Five minutes of walking brings me to the campground, and in 15 minutes I am back at my truck at the lower trailhead by the gate.

Swett Brook Trail is a good choice for a leisurely forest walk over ground with little elevation gain. The variety of forest environments provide a good representation of the conifers and deciduous trees common to the Maine woods. Much to learn along the way! Have a great walk!

Sources for Local Maps

L *Carrabassett Valley Mountain Bike Trail Map:* Sugarloaf Outdoor Center; Maine Huts and Trails Headquarters, Kingfield; High Peaks Information Center, Highway 27, Carrabassett Valley; carrabassett.nemba.org.

L *Maine Huts and Trails System Map:* MHT Headquarters, Kingfield; at individual Huts; at Trailhead signboards/kiosks; High Peaks Information Center, Highway 27, Carrabassett Valley; www.mainehuts.org

L *The Valley Below* (Map of Bigelow Preserve and Flagstaff Lake): High Peaks Information Center, Highway 27, Carrabassett Valley; www.mainehighpeaks.com

L *Rangeley Lakes Heritage Trust Maps:* RLHT Headquarters, Oquossoc; Outfitters in Rangeley; www.rlht.org

L *Bigelow Preserve:* Maine Bureau of Public Lands (search online); maps may be available at MBPL Office. Farmington.

L *Mt. Blue State Park* : Maine Bureau of Public Lands (search online); Park gatehouse; maps may be available at MBPL Office, Farmington.

L Delorme *Maine Atlas:* Usually more suitable for driving access than hiking, as trailheads and hiking trails are not necessarily displayed. Available at outfitters, bookstores, grocery and convenience stores throughout Maine and the region.

Recommended Reading and References

Birds

Birds of Maine Field Guide. (2002). Stan Tekela. Adventure Publications, Inc. Cambridge, MN (2002). 119 Maine birds; color photos; compact size.

National Geographic Birds Phone App: Photos, maps, sounds, appearance, behavior.

Trees

Forest Trees of Maine, Centennial Edition (2008). Maine Forest Service, Department of Agriculture, Conservation, and Forestry—available at book stores and from the Department. All major trees to be found in Maine; color photos; identification tips.

Plants

Wild Plants of Maine: A Useful Guide (Second edition, 2014). Tom Seymour. Just Write Books, Topsham, Maine. A guide to edible (and inedible) wild plants, with photos—and even recipes. Consider the elderberry fritters!

History

Mountains of Maine: Intriguing Stories Behind Their Names (2009). Steven Pinkham. Downeast Books, Camden, Maine. This book fascinates with references to Abnaki history, colorful settlers, and legend. How about "Picked Chicken Hill"? Illustrated with reproductions of old postcards.

Lost Villages of Flagstaff Lake (2010) Alan L. Burnell and Kenny R. Wing. Arcadia Publishing, Charleston, SC. Photographs, old maps, and extensive captions pertaining to life in the communities of Flagstaff, Dead River, and Bigelow before the damming of the Dead River and the creation of Flagstaff Lake.

Verne and Me (2013) and *I'll Be Back, Judith* (2015) H. Coval Conant. Fictionalized accounts of life in Weld, in the 1930s onward, written by one who did exactly that. If you have lived in Weld for a while, you may recognize yourself in this book! Available at Weld stores, other Franklin County outlets, and on-line.

Observation

Pilgrim at Tinker Creek (1974). Annie Dillard. Harpers Magazine Press. This is a classic. Dillard writes of daily visits to the creek near her home in the southern Appalachians. With uncanny eye and ear, she brings the reader along on these visits, with a passion.

Let Us Hear From You!

Have a favorite trail not described here? Have a suggestion? A correction? Have a great time and want to share the good news? Let's hear from you!

footandpaddle@gmail.com

Happy trails!

Photo Credits

All photographs are by Doug Dunlap, unless noted.

Pages 99 and 100 photos by Michael Höhne.